LEGENDEERING

LEGENDEERING

THE BRAND-NEW (BUT TRIED-AND-TRUE) VIDEO COMMUNICATION STRATEGY TO **HUMANIZE** YOUR BUSINESS

TOM LANGAN

WORLDCHANGERS
MEDIA

Hardcover ISBN: 978-1-955811-48-4
Paperback ISBN: 978-1-955811-49-1
E-book ISBN: 978-1-955811-50-7
Library of Congress Control Number: 2023914902

First hardcover edition: September 2023

Layout & Design: Bryna Haynes
Cover Image: @4zevar via AdobeStock
Editors: Bryna Haynes, Paul Baillie-Lane

Published by WorldChangers Media
PO Box 83, Foster, RI 02825
www.WorldChangers.Media

For all the teachers who wrote "not living up to his potential" on my report card.

&

To the countless hours of television I watched as a child. You didn't "rot my brain" or "ruin my eyesight". You inspired this.

PRAISE

"I am so grateful that Tom Langan has written *Legendeering*, a book that holds true to its promise. The tried-and-true strategy he lays out in this book embodies the same principles and philosophies we employed at Nickelodeon to grow from nothing in 1980 to a juggernaut worth $10 billion in just sixteen years. And, while *Legendeering* provides readers with a theoretical understanding of why we work to build legendary brands, this book takes the extra step to arm its readers with a brand-new and pragmatic approach to the how. In a world where young people can smell inauthenticity miles away, *Legendeering* is an essential primer for building brands that they will cherish for years to come."

**Geraldine Laybourne, serial entrepreneur,
former President of Nickelodeon and
co-founder of Oxygen Media**

"Tom Langan writes from the heart with passion and exuberance. With storytelling as a north star and humanity as a guiding principle, this book pilots you in the right direction for success."

Sara Kozak, TV executive

"Through a mix of captivating stories, insightful lessons, and actionable strategies, Tom Langan illustrates the remarkable things that happen when you set out to humanize the world of business. In *Legendeering,* he shows how powerful it is to put people over product, and reminds us that, regardless of what we do for a living, we can all make the choice to be in the hospitality industry."

Will Guidara, celebrated restaurateur, author of *Unreasonable Hospitality*

"Most entrepreneurs (and many businesses for that matter) fail because they give up what they want most for what they want now—they chase short-term revenues over long-term relationships. In *Legendeering,* Tom Langan offers an antidote to this epidemic of extractionary capitalism and gifts us with an alternative, sustainable, and community focused pathway to transform our businesses into brands that matter."

Alok Appadurai, *Wall Street Journal* Bestselling author and founder of Uplift Millions

CONTENTS

PART II: LEGENDEER YOUR CONTENT

Legendeering

Le·gen·deer·ing (*'lɛdʒənd'irɪŋ*); ***vt.***

1. The act of designing and constructing a
    strong and stable framework to create
    engaging, story driven video content;

2. Leveraging the power of storytelling
    through video to engineer rapid business
    growth and foster long lasting and
    meaningful relationships between a
    business and their audience

INTRODUCTION

HI, I'M TOM, and I'm a video production expert.

Before we begin, let me address the elephant in the room: why is a video guy writing a *book* about how to create legendary marketing content with video?

It's ironic, I know. But it also makes sense.

Video is the single most powerful tool businesses have at their disposal. Period. Video builds relationships, creates deep connections, and engages multiple senses to create lasting memories around your message. In fact, businesses that utilize video in their marketing strategies enjoy an average of 49 percent higher revenue growth than those who don't.[1] If you're not using video to connect with your community and get your ideas out there, it's my intention that this book will inspire you to start.

However, one thing you *can't* do with video is leave it open on your desk, scribble in it, dog-ear it, and physically hand it off to friends who are also suffering from marketing burnout.

Like video, a book engages multiple senses (touch, sight, even smell and hearing) to enhance memory and help create connections in the brain.

Like well-produced video content, a book is designed to fulfill a clear expectation. For example, by the time you're done reading *Legendeering*, you'll understand exactly what Legendeering is, why it works, and how to implement it across all of your online channels to deliver value to your community. This, in turn, will help you lay the foundation for lasting, profitable relationships with your customers and clients.

And, like video, a book builds a relationship between author and reader. Like video, it's a conversation. In fact, by the time you turn the last page, I guarantee you'll hear my voice in your head whenever you sit down to post on social media. I'll leave it up to you whether or not that's a good thing.

Finally, if I were to convey all of the information in this book via video, it would be a feature-length piece

1 https://awesome.vidyard.com/rs/273-EQL-130/images/Vidyard_Aberdeen_ Impact_of_Video_Marketing.pdf

of content—and while it would be cool to design and create *Legendeering: The Movie*, it wouldn't be as practical or useful to you as this book.

So, now that we've answered that burning question, let's get down to business.

How to Use This Book

This book is intended to teach you a very specific content development strategy which I have developed and refined. As you may have guessed, that strategy is called "Legendeering."

This strategy involves two parts: the philosophy upon which Legendeering is built, and a multi-phase action path for the creation of long-form, episodic video content according to the core principle and directives of that philosophy.

Let me be clear: Legendeering is *not* a sales framework. I am not a sales expert. Nor am I a marketing expert (at least, not in the way we've come to understand "marketing" in the online world). I'm a content development and communications expert who has applied my 40,000+ hours of experience in TV and commercial development and production to create a pathway for building community around brands—because, in the end, an engaged community is what determines the success and sustainability of any business.

In order to help you be successful with this strategy and adapt it to your business, we need to break down the current conversation about what marketing is, what it isn't, and why all those "expert" hacks, tips, and tricks don't actually work to create long-term success or revenue. That's what we'll be doing in the first part of the book.

In the second part, we'll be looking at implementation. I'll put on my "producer" hat and share the practical steps you'll need to know in order to develop, produce, and distribute your Legendeered video content.

Of course, I wouldn't be a video guy if I didn't have a whole bunch of my own Legendeered video content to share. You'll find links to this content throughout the book, as well as in the Resources section at the back. I also encourage you to join me on my YouTube channel and social media platforms to see exactly how the Legendeering strategy plays out in real time. Think of it as me buying you dinner. (That reference will make more sense later, I promise.)

That said ...

If you're looking to make a quick buck with the latest sparkly online strategy, build an audience of followers with whom you never actually intend to have a conversation, or are 100 percent devoted to your current "sell your ass off in every post" strategy, do us both a favor and put this book down now. That's not what Legendeering is about.

However, if you think most marketing strategies feel more like selling your soul than starting a movement, or if you're tired of every conversation being tied to a transaction, or if you've been asking yourself,

"Why can't there be a better way to get visibility for my business?" then you're in the right place. You're about to learn—or, as you'll discover, *re*learn—a more ethical, authentic, and relationship-based way of marketing your business.

This is marketing the way marketing was always *supposed* to be done.

Core Principle and Directives

The core principle of Legendeering is: "Lead with Value, Always."

That principle is the foundation upon which the entire Legendeering strategy is built—because if you're not leading with value, you're not serving your audience. Period.

Under the umbrella of that core principle are five key directives, which we will be exploring together over the course of this book.

The Key Directives of Legendeering are:

1. Give without expectation
2. Be relentlessly authentic
3. It's not about you. It's about them
4. Start with story, follow up with facts
5. Consistency is key

In keeping with these directives, it is my intention that the stories and discussions in Part I of this book provide you with a lifetime of value by radically shifting the way you think about marketing and how you engage with your community.

In Part II, I'll show you how to operationalize your new knowledge. You'll discover how to leverage natural human tendencies to create authentic relationships based on trust, identify what people in your community need so you can provide value over and above expectations, and, on the technical side, how to develop, produce, and distribute evergreen episodic content that will make you a legend in your niche.

Are you ready to begin? Then turn the page, and let's change your world.

THE LEGENDEERING MAP

CORE PRINCIPLE
LEAD WITH VALUE

Philosophy

- Directive #1: Give without expectation
- Directive #2: Be relentlessly authentic
- Directive #3: It's not about you. It's about them
- Directive #4: Start with story, follow up with facts
- Directive #5: Consistency is key

YOUR STORY

Content Creation

- Phase #1: Development
- Phase #2: Preproduction
- Phase #3: Production
- Phase #4: Postproduction
- Phase #5: Distribution

BECOME LEGENDARY!

Legendeering is marketing the way marketing was always *supposed* to be done.

PART I

LEGENDEER YOUR THINKING

CHAPTER ONE

WHAT MAKES
A LEGEND?

The Value of Story

IT WAS APRIL 25, 2019. After wrapping up a long day of shooting in Boston, I limped back to my hotel room to watch the New York Emmy Awards before catching a few hours of sleep. My better half, Becky, was at home and (as was too often the case) I was not, so we agreed to watch the show together on our laptops and text updates back and forth.

Normally I don't make watching the Emmys a priority, but this time was different. The show I'd worked on a few months before, a lifestyle program called *Her Big Idea*, had been nominated in two categories: *Entertainment: Program Feature/Segment,* and *Lifestyle Program: Program/Special.* A number of us from the team had been named within the nomination, so it felt like a major group triumph.

I set up my laptop on the kitchen counter of my Extended Stay America suite, poured myself a whiskey, and wondered, "If we win, what will change?"

Honestly, I wasn't sure. More funding, maybe? A continuation of the show for a third or fourth season?

I decided that the night felt like a victory regardless of whether we won or not. I'd always be able to add "two-time Emmy Award nominated" to my shirt-tail—and, I had to admit, that was pretty cool.

Most of the text conversation between Becky and me revolved around guessing when one of the categories we were nominated for would come up. There didn't seem to be any rhyme or reason. It was like having a Band-Aid removed as slowly as humanly possible. Finally, after what seemed like hours, they announced the first category we'd placed in; we didn't win, but we still had another shot at bringing home the trophy. I was half asleep by the time they finally got to the next category and announced the winners, who were ...

Not us. Again.

I blew out a breath, expecting to feel disappointed. Instead, what ran through my head was: "Is this it? Is this really what I've been working toward for my entire professional life?"

The truth was, I'd already begun extracting myself from the television industry, specifically from the more demanding aspects of working as a producer and show-runner. I'd been working in that capacity for years, in both major cities and remote locations, and with amazing (and sometimes very quirky) people. But although I was technically in charge of many of the shows I worked on, I had very little creative control. After all, network television of any variety is engineered to draw large, general audiences to get as many eyes as possible on their ads. There was only so much I could do when it came to adding value for the people consuming the programs.

So, I'd decided a few years before to focus more on cinematography. Being a Director of Photography carried a hell of a lot less pressure than being a producer did. I loved my work, particularly the creative story-telling aspects of it. But on the night of the Emmys, as I closed my laptop, climbed into the unfamiliar hotel bed, and lay staring into the dark, it was clear I was no longer fulfilled by it.

It's funny how, by the time we make our big dreams a reality, we no longer want them in the same way. I felt like I'd spent the last seventeen years climbing a ladder, only to get a few rungs from the top, look around, and realize I didn't even like the view.

However, I digress.

Those Emmy nominations were the beginning of the end of my television career. I decided that if I wasn't motivated by that level of prestige and recognition, it was probably time to move on. I started asking myself, "If television was no longer an option for me, what would I do instead?

The answer was clear: I'd radically change the way people and brands market through video. Because the way we are doing it is wrong.

It's All for a Good Story

One of the things I loved about working on *Her Big Idea* was the way the show highlighted the stories of women entrepreneurs in a balanced, inspirational way. It was fun to get to know these dynamic women who had created such ripples in their niches. The content was real, the drama minimal. It was a celebration of real success and the real women who had earned it.

However, most of the other shows I worked on were not like that. Honestly, they felt like cheesy clickbait dressed up for television. The most prevalent questions being asked by those in charge were, "Where's the drama? What are the stakes? How can we put so-and-so in jeopardy this week?" Of course, the subtext to this discussion was: *How can we get those Nielsen ratings up? How much can we sell commercial slots for? How much revenue will this show make for us in the next few months?*

Spoiler alert: there is almost nothing genuine or authentic about reality television, on any network, with any subject matter. The impetus behind all of those shows is to garner as much attention as possible, because more attention means higher ratings. In the TV business model, ratings are the only thing that matter, because ratings equal ad revenue, and ad revenue is how television networks make money. The whole model is built on *what draws attention*—and it doesn't matter whether that attention is positive or negative. No significance is assigned to whether the show is making a contribution to, or moving the needle for, the viewer. In fact, almost no one seems to care whether or not the story is actually worth telling, as long as it keeps people coming back.

In many ways, we are regurgitating the TV ratings model in the business space, through the vehicle of social media. Instead of asking, "Will this video/post serve my audience (and, by extension, my business)?" we're asking, "How many likes/views will this get?" Just like in the broadcast television world, there's a perception that views outweigh value when it comes to financial return. Worst of all, this idea is supported by those in the marketing industry who traffic in "impressions" on social media. Impressions are the Nielsen ratings of social media and, just like views in the television world, they're a junk metric.

But here's the thing. Stories—and the connections that stories build—are *the only thing* that moves the needle in business, in relationships, and even in our inner worlds. The stories we tell, the stories we watch and listen to, the stories we read ... these shape our view of life, the world, and one another. They *matter*.

More, stories are our most powerful pathway for learning. According to many leading anthropologists, storytelling—specifically, the ability to pass on generational wisdom in a memorable way through the medium of story—played a crucial role in our evolution as a species.[2]

So, when I decided in 2019 that my television career was over for good, I started looking at how we use story in other formats—and, in particular, how leveraging story to deliver massive value can take a brand from mediocre to legendary.

Value Is the Only Metric That Matters

Imagine yourself walking up to a stranger on the street, sticking out your hand, and saying, "Hi! I'm [your name]. I make widgets. My widgets cost $100. So, get out your wallet, give me $100, and I'll give you one of these super awesome and shiny widgets."

Even in your imagination, you would never do that. It's gross. You intuitively know that this approach does not work.

And yet, that's the basic premise of most sales and marketing. From network television to social media, and from magazine ads to that all-important countertop space at your favorite chain coffee house, everyone everywhere is pitching, pitching, pitching. Wherever we go, we are being sold to—with or without our consent. We're bombarded with images, offers, and promises without ever getting more than a cursory introduction to the brand, the people behind it, or the values they espouse.

---

2 https://www.nature.com/articles/s41467-017-02036-8 and https://www.news-week.com/storytelling-human-evolution-society-organized-religion-739585

Our relationships, even with the brands we buy from on a regular basis, are generally transactional. They want our money; we want their stuff. An exchange occurs, and that's the end of it—at least, until the next ad pops up.

Consumers are sick of it. Business owners are sick of it. Even career marketers are sick of it. And I'll be willing to bet that you're sick of it, too.

Consider that sinking feeling in your gut when you tack your stale pitch onto yet another story-based social media post (because "people buy stories!"). Think of how yucky it feels to always be selling and never just sharing. Think of how disappointed you get when yet another launch or visibility campaign returns lackluster results, even though you "did everything right." Think of how cold-calling sets your stomach turning or makes you want to hide under your desk.

Many coaches and business experts would tell you that you feel that way because you have a poor money mindset, or that your offer isn't aligned, or that "you just need to learn to love selling." They'd tell you that the issue isn't the way you're doing things, it's you. *You* are the problem because you don't want to sell like everyone else. *You* are the barrier between your business and the amazing, reciprocal relationships you dream of having with your clients and customers.

They're wrong.

Let me be clear: there's nothing inherently bad about sales. That's how economies work, how businesses succeed, how employees get paid, and how consumers get the goods they need to survive and thrive. The problem, rather, is with *how we've been trained to sell*. Those tried-and-true methods rely on engineered needs to generate transactional exchanges. They are all quantity and no quality. That approach doesn't just offend our integrity, it goes against our innate humanity.

Over the last forty years or so, we have been taught to value short-term profits above all else. In pursuit of that goal, we began to treat our customers like data points on sales reports and dollars on balance sheets rather than like the actual human beings they are.

Legendeering, the strategy we're going to explore together in this book, is my answer to the soulless, valueless, predatory content inundating every form of media today. It's not a new approach, per se, except in its application across our modern platforms; nor is it a fad marketing formula. It's a long-term approach to visibility and content marketing that aligns with our humanity, our affinity for story, and our desire for real relationships. More, it can enable any business, of any size, in any industry, to attract an aligned audience of raving fans, become a standout authority in their niche, and create a truly legendary brand.

Put simply, Legendeering is the strategy of leveraging long-form video communication to deliver value to your target audience and create a "mythos" around your brand that fosters real, reciprocal relationships between you and your customers and clients. It builds community around your brand, and it works *without*

*you needing to push, position, or pitch a single product
or service.*

Yes, Legendeering empowers brands to create
massive upticks in sales by ... not selling.

Hear me out.

SERVE FIRST, SELL SECOND

Brands become legends not because of the products
or services they sell, but because of the stories that
grow up around them. Think of Apple and you likely
picture Steve Jobs (and recall at least one story about
his sometimes-tyrannical reign in Apple's top office).
On a smaller scale, think of the legendary businesses
in your hometown and the stories you tell about them.
No one goes to the dive bar on Main Street for the
atmosphere—and yet, the place is always packed. No
matter what your original Saturday plans, you find
yourself drawn back there again and again, despite
the sticky floors and the questionable smudges on the
pint glasses.

You don't buy from Apple because what they sell
is inherently better, but because of the feelings and
stories you associate with the brand. Nor do you go to
the dive bar because they serve the best beer. I mean,
you can drink cheap beer anywhere—why go to the
place that smells like an old shoe and has a single,
half-functional toilet? Think about it. You go for the
stories—for the nostalgia of Saturdays past, for the
kooky owner who likes to show off his ceramic dog

collection, and for the bartender's war stories. You go there because of the people behind the brand, and the relationship you have with them.

If we marry story with value—and by "value," I mean value for the consumer—we create something even more epic. Tom's Shoes is inseparable from its brand story of "buy a pair, give a pair," even though, as of 2019, the company is no longer giving away shoes as part of its philanthropy. People are willing to pay more at Tom's because they like being part of that giving narrative. Stories about how doTerra's manufacturing practices support indigenous communities and sustainable agriculture are not only motivating and validating for its independent salespeople but also a huge draw for consumers of essential oils and personal care products. The value that both these companies deliver is wrapped up in personal, heartwarming, human tales—and it keeps paying off.

That's why I framed the core principle of Legendeering as four simple words:

Lead. With. Value. *Always.*

It's simple, and also profound. To truly lead with value is so far from the norm of modern marketing that it feels counterintuitive. And yet, once you implement what you're about to learn in this book, not only will you completely eliminate your adversarial feelings around marketing, you will also significantly increase your profits, visibility, and brand recognition.

If you deliver value, people will buy. It's been true since the dawn of commerce, and it's still true today.

Of course, there are many nuances to be explored at this complex intersection of value and story—and we'll be delving into all of them in this book. For now, though, I want you to ask yourself one simple question:

What stories do *you* want to tell?

CHAPTER TWO

LET ME BUY YOU DINNER

The Rule of Reciprocation

I WAS WORKING on a project in Detroit when I got a call from a friend and former boss. He was working on a new show for The Weather Channel with Al Roker Entertainment.

"So, Tom," he began. "How soon can you get to Alaska? I need you ASAP."

He explained that he was working on a show called *Coast Guard: Alaska* and needed a showrunner and series producer to deal with the complex logistics of working, filming, and managing a team in one of the world's most challenging environments.

I'm never one to back down from a challenge—
and, quite frankly, the pawn shop series I was filming
at the time was less than inspiring.

Of course, my immediate reply was, "I can be on a
plane in two weeks."

And that was how I ended up spending the next
two years in Alaska.

We got off to a rocky start. There were a lot of complicated variables to juggle, particularly in the field.
We were operating at the intersection of the Coast
Guard apparatus, the men and women who serve in
the Guard, the communities they support, and our
task to document and tell their stories. We had permanent crews in two locations, satellite crews during
the (slightly) warmer summer months, and winter
crews in some of the Coast Guard's forward operating
positions around the state.

We worked closely with the Coast Guard to document all aspects of their work. Sometimes our crews
went out on cutters; sometimes they flew on aerial
search and rescue missions. I got to go to a lot of places
I never thought I'd see, and do a lot of things that,
looking back, were both exciting and terrifying.

On a warm August night (by Alaskan standards,
at least) our Kodiak-based film crew were fast asleep
in our lodge when we were awoken by the emergency
pager—a one-way radio commonly used by first
responders. The alarm tones sounded, and over the
pager we heard the announcement from the OOD
(Officer of the Day) at the air station: "Fishing vessel

taking on water approximately fourteen miles south-east of Old Harbor"—which put it about fifty miles from Coast Guard Air Station Kodiak.

I roused the crew, banging on doors and shouting, "We've got a search and rescue call!" Minutes later, we were racing to the hangar.

One of our crew got on the helicopter with the Coast Guard crew. It was the darkest part of the short summer night. Even with an approximate location, it was going to be hard to pinpoint a sinking ship in the vast Gulf of Alaska.

I learned from my crew member later that, by the time the helicopter arrived, the ship was already completely submerged. Three crew members were shivering in the life raft. One, whose name was Jaime, had gone down with the boat.

The surviving crew members were whisked away by ambulance to the local hospital as soon as the helicopter touched down in Kodiak. Two of the crew were hypothermic and one, despite the best efforts of the Coast Guard Rescue Swimmer who administered CPR in the helicopter, later passed away at the hospital. In all the chaos, no one seemed to know what had happened to the boat. Had it struck something? Had there been a mechanical malfunction? It had all happened so fast.

We reverted to our documentary instincts as, over the course of the next eighteen hours, the Coast Guard launched four additional helicopters and one C-130 to continue the search for Jaime, the missing crew member. Despite their best efforts, he was never found.

We had the makings of a compelling story, but even from our place on the periphery, the human cost was heartbreaking. Jaime was officially declared "lost at sea."

In the days that followed, my team managed to track down the contact information of the owners of the vessel who, with permission, connected us with the remaining crew members. He also gave us the phone number of Amy, Jaime's fiancée. We let the owners know that we'd follow up within the week.

About five days later, I reached out to Amy to let her know we had documented the rescue of Jaime's crewmates. Mostly, I didn't want her to be surprised or traumatized if she saw the episode on television.

"I can't even imagine what you're dealing with," I told her. "This is a terrible time. But I also want you to know that if there's ever anything you want to share about Jaime, we are more than happy to listen."

We didn't schedule an interview on that call—and honestly, I didn't expect her to want to talk to us at all. However, she called me back just a couple of days later, and said, "I'm ready."

"I can't promise this will be on the show," I warned her. "But I can promise that we will listen, and that we'll give you an opportunity to tell your story, and his. And I will do everything I can to make sure it makes it on to the show, so people can know who Jaime was and what he meant to you and your children."

The interview took place in our main base of operations, a six-bedroom lodge a few miles from the Coast Guard base in Kodiak. We sipped coffee and I walked her through the structure of the interview while the crew set up the lighting. Then, it was time to get rolling.

By the time Amy was done speaking, there wasn't a dry eye in the room. It was a beautiful tribute to the person she would no longer get to spend the rest of her life with. In fact, it was one of the most emotional pieces I've ever filmed.

In television production, you're often working in a vacuum. You run into people who might know about the shows you've done, but the only people who really get the day-in, day-out experience are the people on your crew. The audience—and, by extension, the broader impact of what you're sharing through the program—can feel hard to access. Often, the audience has a completely different experience of the material than those who are actually producing it.

That day in Kodiak, I felt a renewed sense of obligation around my work. We weren't just telling a powerful story; we were creating someone's legacy and sharing it with the world. I'd always known we had the power to do that, but this particular story drove it home in a much bigger, more visceral way. The experience of telling these stories of life and death shifted my priorities; for the first time in my career, I started to focus on creating a positive impact.

After I left the show in 2013, I continued to keep in touch with Amy. Every so often, she'd check in with me to see how life was going, and fill me in on how things were evolving for her. Each time we talked, she thanked me for helping her tell her story, and for helping Jaime's life to be remembered in a meaningful way. The more we spoke, the more I felt that sense of purpose and obligation grow.

When I decided to leave television for good in 2019, I again remembered the inescapable gravity of that interview. That day, we hadn't been a television crew. We'd simply been humans witnessing another human in her grief, pride, and uncertainty. We'd built a relationship through her story, and it was powerful.

Relationships Are *Everything*

Often, television crews are actively discouraged from forming connections with the people we are filming. In situations where we're working with real people (not actors), we are encouraged to act like we care while simultaneously keeping a "responsible" distance. It's very duplicitous. The goal of the film crew is always to get a performance out of the subjects—but to the subjects, it's all real life, and they're seeking support and connection to weather it. The result is nearly always some form of physical, emotional, or circumstantial exploitation.

If you're thinking, "That is messed up on *so* many levels," you're right.

But if you're also thinking that this is unique to the television industry, you're sadly mistaken. Television and media are certainly the most obvious examples of "performance for profit"—but, in fact, it happens everywhere in marketing.

How many times have you been drawn to a company or individual because of how they presented themselves ... only to find out (after you'd handed over your credit card, of course) that they weren't quite who you thought they were? It's almost expected that companies will misrepresent themselves in some way in their marketing—by exaggerating, posturing, or even outright fibbing. (Don't even get me started on all those "influencers" posing on other people's Lamborghinis when they can't pay their rent.)

The solution to this, of course, is simple, at least in concept: stop trying to cultivate an image, and be exactly who you are, all the time. Only from there can authentic relationships be built, nurtured, and expanded.

In practice, however, this is more complex. Being transparent, vulnerable, and authentic—particularly in a public-facing way—goes against everything most of us have been taught about business. Despite modern advances in work culture (work from home, anyone?) there is still a widespread belief that you have to be a "professional" version of yourself at work and reserve your "real" self for behind closed doors.

I don't know about you, but my "business face" doesn't automatically switch off at 5:00 p.m. and turn back again at 9:00 a.m. I am who I am, and quite frankly, I'm not willing to expend the effort to be anyone else.

Sure, we need boundaries in professional settings. Spilling your guts about your relationship troubles to a client you just met? Not good. Charging thousands of dollars to your expense account to treat your family on vacation? Also not good—and potentially criminal. But boundaries around behavior don't need to equal boundaries around personality and expression. To expect individuals or teams to, at best, put on a Photoshop-worthy gloss every day—and at worst, outright pretend to be people they're not—in order to operate in a business setting is ridiculous, exhausting, and a terrible way to go through life. More, it's unsustainable. No one can keep up an act during every waking hour. Sooner or later, the mask will slip, and when that happens, any trust that has been built will come tumbling down like a Jenga tower. It's a question of when, not if.

This mentality around presenting an "upgraded" version of ourselves pervades online and entrepreneurial spaces, too—only, instead of having a persona imposed on us by an organization, we're doing it to ourselves. Instagram filters. Selective storylines. Humble brags. "Never let 'em see you sweat." These all create overly polished narratives that attract buyers but have little or nothing to do with reality. Think broke business coaches teaching "How to Make Your First Million in Ten Days," marketing gurus who can't build an audience, and naturally slim twenty-somethings hocking "miracle" diet pills. If it's too good to be true, it probably is. And yet, even as consumers become ever savvier and more cynical, the culture of hype persists.

Business is powered by *relationships*. When those relationships are built on mutual trust, authenticity, and shared values, they thrive. When they are built on pretense, swagger, and false connections, they combust—sometimes to the tune of millions of dollars and hundreds of jobs.

I don't believe most of us want this false face. We don't want to have to pretend to be who we are not. We don't want to build a house of cards. We want true community and true connection—and yet, we aren't presented with many examples of authentic values creating profit. So, we do what everyone else is doing, and wonder why it doesn't work for us.

That said, it's true that dollars flow toward hype— and there's a reason for this. It's called *negativity bias*. We are biologically programmed to pay attention to things that seem adverse, threatening, or dangerous. For thousands of years, this programming helped us avoid predation to survive and reproduce. But although most of us no longer have to worry about animal ambushes in our daily lives, we still tend to focus on the negative. If you pay attention, you'll see that most business fads are, in one way or another, tapped into this negativity bias. There's something that feels immediate or threatening embedded in the message, and people eat it up. There's also the very real phenomena of intentional negative press and clickbait practices. Too often, when profits are involved, it's a race to the bottom.

Ever heard the term FOMO (Fear of Missing Out)? The key word, of course, is fear; this approach uses our negativity bias to garner attention, and companies use it to sell to us constantly. (Think of all the times you've seen an ad or piece of content from a business using phrases like "For a limited time only" or "While supplies last!") These sales techniques are pervasive—but what we often don't see is that, once the hype is exposed, those dollars flow just as quickly away. As growth strategies, pretense, scarcity, and fear are unsustainable. There are better ways to get attention if you're willing to play a long game.

THE PEAK END RULE

Real relationships in business are not transactional, even when they include transactional elements. They aren't dependent on our clients and customers doing what we want them to, when we want them to, but rather on mutual trust and respect. Therefore, they can endure even when circumstances change. Relationships turn curious parties into buyers, and buyers into raving fans.

We didn't interview Amy because we wanted to coax a performance out of her. We simply wanted to tell her story—and the result was a relationship that spanned years, long after I left *Coast Guard: Alaska*. She felt seen, heard, and cared for—and reciprocated accordingly with her own care and attention. In fact, ten years later, we are still connected; I am one of only 200 people she follows on Instagram.

When you have a relationship of mutual trust and respect with a person or organization, you will forgive them their mistakes. You will try again when things get hard. You will work with them toward a solution rather than bailing at the first sign of trouble. You will invest in them because you know that they are, in some way, invested in you—that you *matter* to them.

This may sound unrealistic in a business context, but it's actually not. After all, businesses are built and run by people; you cannot separate the two. According to a phenomenon called the Peak End Rule, a series of high points in a relationship or experience will outweigh negative moments—even after our negativity bias is accounted for. Quite simply, positive memories—particularly those created through relationships—are more powerful than negative reactions.

Let's look at this more closely.

Imagine that you've just been seated at an upscale restaurant with your best friend. (Note: you'll soon see that all my best analogies are food-related. Bear with me.)

You're totally pumped for this meal, for a whole host of reasons. You order the meal you've dreamed of for weeks—and yet, when the food comes out, the dish that lands in front of you is not what you ordered. There's been a mix-up; you ordered a steak, but there's fish on your plate.

This, I'm sure you can agree, is a negative experience. The more anticipated the meal, the bigger the disappointment when your expectations aren't met.

The waiter apologizes profusely. "I am so sorry. I will get your steak out to you immediately." In the meantime, another round of drinks is ordered. More apologies are issued. And when your steak arrives, it is perfectly cooked.

If the food is as good as I'm imagining it to be, the meal alone might overwrite the memory of the initial mix-up. But now imagine that, when you raise your head after devouring your steak (having successfully resisted the urge to lick the plate clean), you notice the manager walking toward you with a cocktail tray.

"Please accept our most sincere apologies for the issues with your meal," she says. "This round of drinks is on the house, and we'd love to treat you to dessert as well."

By this point, you have not only forgiven the restaurant for its mistake, but you're also feeling like royalty.

Later, when you tell your friends about your experience, you'll probably mention the fish-instead-of-steak mix-up, but your overall focus will be on how the complimentary cocktails came at just the right time, how utterly awesome that free dessert was, and how the whole staff generally went out of their way to make your night divine. In fact, there's a better-than-average chance that you'll visit that restaurant again.

Now, imagine instead that the waiter had refused to apologize, and no attempt was made to correct the restaurant's mistake. As a result, you and your friend spent the entire meal complaining to each other about the terrible service. What story would you tell about the restaurant then?

The Peak End Rule applies in all kinds of business scenarios, from hospitality to product sales, salon visits to consulting gigs, online tech to live events—in fact, to *any experience that has a clear beginning and end*. However, in order for an experience to overcome negativity bias, it must create positive highlights or "peaks" and end on a positive note.

In our restaurant example, the peaks (the overall ambiance, the character of the waiter and manager, and the perfectly cooked steak) overwhelmed the negativity of the incorrect entrée. The positive ending to the night—courtesy of the complimentary cocktails and delicious dessert—left you with a good taste in your mouth (pun intended) even after potentially catastrophic mistakes were made.

Ultimately, the Peak End Rule only works if you understand what your customers and community value. At the restaurant, they understood that you valued good food, good service, and accountability. Because the staff at the restaurant understood those values, and shared them in common with you, they were able to turn a negative moment into a positive experience. On the flip side, if you don't work to understand your customers—your *community*—as human beings, the opportunity to utilize the Peak End Rule to overcome negativity bias will never materialize.

We'll discuss values and how to share them effectively later in this book. But for now, understand this: shared values plus authentic expression of those values equals trust. And trust wins every time.

Everyone Loves a Giver

Different from the Peak End Rule, but equally important to authentic business relationships, is the Rule of Reciprocation.

Imagine that you're out to dinner (again) with your friend, Joe. At the end of the meal, Joe whips out his credit card and says, "I got this. Dinner is on me."

How do you feel?

Unless you're a total mooch, you immediately say, "You don't have to do that. Let me split the check with you, or at least cover the drinks." But Joe insists and will not be swayed, so you accept his gift with a heartfelt, "Wow, thanks!" immediately followed by, "I've got the next one."

Again, unless you're a mooch, Joe's generosity likely made such an impact on you that you make it a point to return the favor. At the end of your next meal together, you sneak off and hand the server your card to make *absolutely sure* you get to pay the bill this time around. After all, you wouldn't want to miss the chance to <u>reciprocate</u>!

Why do we do this? Because the Rule of Reciprocation is programmed into us from the time we are babies. It is part of the social contract that we follow in all our interactions. In its most simple form, the Rule of Reciprocation states: "You cannot take [receive] without giving in return."

We begin teaching our children to say "thank you" when given something even before they learn to speak, because saying thank you is how you demonstrate gratitude when given a gift. When we pass a stranger on the street and they say, "Good morning," we say, "Good morning!" It's reflexive. From cards to compliments, meals to social media shares, and everything in between, we cannot receive without giving in return. This rule permeates all of our interpersonal relationships, from birth through death—and, I would argue, is one of the cornerstones upon which human civilization is built.

So, how does the Rule of Reciprocation work from a marketing standpoint?

It's all about *leading with value.*

(I told you the value thing was important.)

Just like your friends, your customers will want to buy you dinner if you buy them dinner first. When you lead with value, people will reciprocate with value—whether in the form of a purchase, a direct referral, or just a good word. But when a person or business keeps ringing the register without providing reciprocal value for customers, they become like that guy in your friend group who *never* pays for dinner. Maybe he has enough redeeming qualities that you put up with him—but when his credit card never makes it out of his wallet, it's hard not to feel anything but resentful.

If our friendships can't survive mooching, why should business be any different?

Tribe and Prejudice

"Okay," you may be thinking. "I get all of this on a theoretical level. But how do I build relationships that actually translate into sales?"

I'll make this really simple.

Your first job, as someone selling something in a marketplace, is to make your community give a shit about you.

That means *you* have to give a shit about them, what they want, and why they want it—because, reciprocity.

People spend money on things they need, things that make them feel a certain way, things they care about, and things that support their image of themselves—aka, their values. So, unless you legitimately have a product that everyone needs, no one can live without, and no one else can produce or sell (which, by the way, you don't because that doesn't exist), people will only participate in a business relationship with you if they can get on board with who you are and what you represent. This means that, in order to set the stage for long-term success, you must learn to communicate in a language of *shared values*.

One company that has done this really well is Dollar Shave Club. They didn't reinvent the wheel. They simply recognized that there was an entire base of customers whose values didn't align with drugstore razors. People were sick of spending $20 (shared value of choice) for razorblades that only lasted a month (shared value of quality). The founders saw a problem and decided to solve it in a way that was relatable, funny, and irreverent (shared value of humor), and that also provided a viable, high-quality solution for real people.

It seems so silly to have to say, "We should treat our customers like human beings." But for many companies, this reminder is needed. When you get to a certain point, customers can become nothing more than data points on a chart. But even if you never meet them face to face, they're still people who want to be seen, heard, and respected—and who will, individually and collectively, go out of their way to support the people they like and the businesses those people represent.

My longtime friend Will Guidara, a celebrated restaurateur who led the transformation of Eleven Madison Park from a middling New York City bistro into the number-one restaurant in the world, believes that this rift can actually be attributed to the ubiquitous business adage, "What gets measured gets managed." In a recent conversation, Will told me, "Just because you can't measure something doesn't mean it doesn't matter. In fact, in most cases it means that it matters *more*."

Listen to Will. Will is absolutely right.

We are taught in business that everything has to be quantified into a numerical value so it can be tracked on a spreadsheet and evaluated on a P&L. But the most important things to success in business, and in life for that matter, can't be boiled down to numbers—as the Beatles famously said, "Money can't buy me love."

At this point, we are all aware that the mega-corporations we buy from every day don't give a shit about who we are. Our hopes, our dreams, and our challenges mean little or nothing to them. All that matters is that you keep clicking that "Buy Now" button. They might play to shared values of accessibility, ease, convenience, and low prices—but, in my mind, those values aren't strong enough to sustain a relationship through adversity. (Do you have any friendships built on those particular values? I don't.) In fact, I believe that *not one* of the giants we see in retail and tech spaces today are hundred-year corporations. I'd be surprised if many of them survive the next decade in their present form. Why? Because while they're great at short-term profitability, you can't build a legacy on a money grab. More, it's impossible to thrive for that long without interacting with your customers—something that many organizations are doing their best to avoid.

Bottom line: while these giants might have market share today, they don't inspire the kind of loyalty that translates to longevity.

Humans are designed to thrive in community, and communities are nothing more than interconnected networks of—you guessed it—relationships. And while "building a community" has become synonymous in some spaces with "building a following," the two are not the same. One is active, the other passive. One is relationship-focused, the other transactional.

So, if you find yourself getting discouraged because X company is dominating the market share in your industry, don't despair. Instead, look at the places where you will *always* have the advantage: human relationships. Be the place where people don't come just to click "Buy Now," but the place they come to feel seen, heard, and included—and yes, also buy stuff.

Do Unto Others ...

Maya Angelou famously said, "People will forget what you said, people will forget what you did, but people will *never* forget how you made them feel."

As you know, the core principle of Legendeering is: "Lead with Value, Always." The first directive under the umbrella of that principle is: "Give without expectation."

Another way to think of this is, "Provide the value to others that you want to receive for yourself." (I know it's a bit Biblical, but there's a reason the whole "do unto others" adage has stuck around this long.)

When you lead with value, you're leading with an invitation to connect. When you *deliver* that value, you sow the seeds of a relationship. Do that enough times and you begin to build a community. When you and the members of your community exchange value following the Rule of Reciprocation, you create opportunities for you, your business, and the entire community to benefit. You create a rising tide that lifts all boats.

One person who has done this really well is serial entrepreneur Gary Vaynerchuk. When he first joined

Twitter, he replied to every single comment on his tweets. More, he commented on every *share* of his tweets. He took the time to engage with his community, which ensured that they knew he valued their attention. It was a huge investment of time and effort, but today, he has a brand with a fiercely loyal community base and several multi-hundred-million-dollar companies. I'd say it worked.

Here's how Will Guidara describes it: "I give because I know and expect that the act of giving is going to make me happy. When you create a culture of hospitality, it's a win-win-win. First, it's great for the customers you're serving because they feel seen and understood, and feel a sense of belonging. Second, it's a win for the bottom line. When you create a culture of hospitality, the business will become more profitable because of the loyalty you engender from investing in those relationships. And third, it's a win for you and the entire team of people you work with because there's nothing more energizing than seeing the look on someone's face when they receive a gift you are responsible for giving them."

This approach isn't rocket science. It doesn't take years to implement. It doesn't even require face-to-face interaction. But it *does* require a commitment to take off the mask, shuck the false pretenses and Instagram sparkle, and show up authentically according to who you are and what you value. In today's messy marketing world, those things aren't always easy—but they are always worth it. When you do them well, you can become more than just successful. You can become *legendary*.

CHAPTER THREE

TRUST ME

How to be Relentlessly Authentic

I'M GOING TO TELL you a very important story in two versions.

Version 1: The Social Media Edit

Hey friends! I landed my first $50,000 client just months after launching Talex Media. Want to learn how I did it? Drop me a DM!

Version 2: The Real Story

During the spring of my senior year in college, I started looking for a job. I had decided not to go to graduate school, and there wasn't much opportunity in the job market for someone with only a Bachelor's in psychology. Then, a few months before graduation, a phone call changed the course of my life.

A good friend of mine, whom I'd known since high school, called to catch up. I started moaning that my parents were getting on my case about finding a job since they weren't going to support me post-graduation. She suggested, "Why don't you call my dad?"

Her dad just happened to own a television production company. He was launching a new show and was looking for people to fill entry-level "production assistant" positions. Intrigued, I reached out—and was immediately hired. I ran errands, took lunch orders, and hauled gear cases around. Basically, my job was to "assist" the production crew in any way necessary. I loved it.

That was the start of my career in television. I went from doing odd jobs on set to running things as a series producer and showrunner. Pretty cool outcome for a near-accident. But I digress ...

Seventeen years later, I quit the television world and launched Talex Media. The younger brother of that same friend, who was now working for a high-caliber public relations firm, called me a few months into my

*new venture. "I heard you're doing your own
thing now. That's awesome! I have a client
who wants to do a high-end video project—
are you interested?"*

Of course, I said yes immediately.

*Over the course of several projects, that
client has paid me more than $50,000.*

Chances are, you've seen multiple iterations of
the first story splashed across your social media feed.
Product sales brags, coaching brags, and service
brags are everywhere. In a way, it makes sense: (true)
stories about success build credibility. However, what
we often don't see is that, behind every one of those
stories, there's a complex network of relationships.

In fact, I would assert that *every success we create
in business* is, in some way, a direct product of our
relationships.

Sometimes, those relationships are nurtured
purely online—through video, social media posts,
and advertising. Sometimes, they're built in more
formal business or networking settings like master-
minds, industry and professional associations, and
alumni groups. And sometimes, they happen on a
purely personal level through family, friends, neighbors, random bartenders, and the parents you meet in
your kid's school pick-up queue. For me, and for many
of the people in my world, the biggest business break-
throughs often come through personal channels in
the form of referrals.

As we say in New York, "I got a guy."

That's me. I'm the guy they've got.

We buy things from people we know, like, and trust. End of story. And while popular marketing models might focus on things like customer pain points, outcomes, and aspirational emotions, the truth is, we only buy based on those things *when we don't already have a relationship with a human who can provide them.*

We buy from giant corporations because of convenience, availability, and sometimes their brand story. But let's be real: if you personally knew someone who sold toilet paper, phone chargers, or garden hoses—and you actually liked, trusted, and shared values with that person—you'd be far more likely to purchase those items from them, even if they cost a bit more. Genuine relationships based in "know, like, and trust" will always supersede other factors, including price.

My friend's brother could have called any number of talented video production people in the New York area. But when his client needed help, he called *me*. Why? It wasn't because I was the cheapest, the most convenient, or the best-known. He chose to work with me because he personally knew me. He understood my values and how they overlapped with his. He was confident that the materials I produced for his client would be in alignment with the quality his clients expected from *him*. In this respect, I became *an extension of him* in his business. He trusted me to represent him and his company, and to do the job well. Then, when I produced a product the client was thrilled with, my friend got to share in the glory of a job well done.

That's the real juice in how relationships work. It's all about *trust*.

Based on the above example, you might be tempted to think that this trust-based referral system only applies in business-to-business contexts. That would be untrue.

Think of the (probably hundreds of) times you've clicked through to an online store from a Facebook or Instagram ad. You saw products and services that align with who you are and how you want to be perceived. The branding told you a story. You liked the story—and by extension, the company—but you still weren't sure if you wanted or needed the product, so you clicked out of the ad and kept scrolling. Then, a few days later, the all-knowing algorithms showed you a video of the founder of that same company speaking about her commitment to preserving rainforests or paying fair wages or supporting school music programs. Suddenly, that product you didn't actually need became a whole lot more attractive because you now had a personal relationship with the founder—a relationship that felt stronger and more trustworthy because it was built on shared values.

The founder *wasn't directly selling you anything*; she was just sharing her passion for uplifting the world through her products. And you bought it. Literally.

It may seem on the surface like the Facebook ad led to that purchase. Ad managers and marketing gurus would certainly like you to think so. But it wasn't the Facebook ad. It was the *content* of the ad, and the relationship that that content built.

Now, think of how many times you've purchased a product because a friend recommended it. You didn't buy that face cream, those quick-dry shorts, or that top-of-the-line camping gear because you liked it more than any other product out there. Chances are, you didn't even research other products extensively. You bought it because someone you know, like, and trust recommended it. Your friend became, through that referral, *an extension of the business being recommended.* Their relationship with the company became your relationship, too. At that moment, whether you were fully conscious of it or not, you became part of that business's community. And if that business continued to grow that sense of community through their marketing, messaging, and communications, you probably went on to buy more products from them, and to tell *your* friends about them.

Companies who create long-term success all have one thing in common: they are great at building community. When you do business with them, you are automatically included in a group of people who are like you in some way. You share values. You share interests. You share needs, desires, and dreams. Even if it's only for a few minutes while you are clicking "add to cart" on sports gear made entirely from recycled water bottles, you *belong.*

In a global marketplace where entire businesses,

relationships, and experiences can play out in the digital realm without a single instance of actual face time, cultivating that sense of belonging with your audience is not only helpful, it's essential.

Build Trust to Build Your Business

Directive #2 in the Legendeering strategy is: "Be relentlessly authentic." As we've discovered in this chapter, trust *always* wins—and you can't build trust on false faces or exaggerated pretenses.

When you practice relentless authenticity with your community over time, they will grow to trust you. Trust is how businesses are built and sustained.

When you invite reciprocity by delivering consistent value (Directive #1) and deliver that value with relentless authenticity (Directive #2), you *will* become the person or brand to which people who share your values immediately gravitate. You will become the product or provider people trust and return to, over and over, even when bright, shiny new things are on offer.

As we've discovered, much of the marketing conversation revolves around ways to "shortcut" the process of delivering value, nurturing relationships, and building community. These tips, tricks, and "hacks" promise to make the process of getting customers faster and easier. But they also have the effect of taking you—and by extension, your relationship to your community—out of the equation. You don't build relationships through transactional marketing. You might get customers, but unless you can nurture them using the directives you're learning in this book, you are unlikely to keep them.

Let's be real: there's nothing fancy or glamorous about Legendeering. None of the principles and directives we're exploring, or the content development strategies I will share later in this book, are "new" ideas; in fact, most of them are as old as commerce itself. I've simply innovated new ways to apply them in our digital world. Trust has been the heart and soul of business since the dawn of time; just because technology has revolutionized communication doesn't mean it has erased the need for, and people's desire for, trust-based relationships. In fact, I would argue that social media has made the need for authenticity and trust even more pressing.

So, how do you build real relationships without face time?

The answer is simple: through video.

Specifically, through video content designed to showcase your authenticity, create trust, and draw in people who share your values.

YOU HAVE TO SHOW UP TO HAVE A SHOT

I'm a video guy. Obviously.

However, the reason why video content is the heart of the Legendeering strategy is not because of my personal preference. It's because, as I shared in the Introduction, video is by far the best tool we have for building authentic relationships in the digital space.

If you own a business or work for one, you almost certainly have access to the tools you need to connect with your community through video. I don't know a single successful businessperson—in the developed world, at least—who doesn't have a smartphone and a laptop with a webcam. Those tools are pretty much prerequisites at this point.

And yet, a shockingly small percentage of businesses are using video as their primary means of communicating with their communities.

It's my mission to change that. Because video *works*.

In a recent study, participants were presented with simple information in two formats. One was text only. The other was video. The participants who only read the text retained just 10 percent of the information. Given how much text we read in an average day, this is hardly surprising.

But those who were shown a video? They retained *95 percent* of what was communicated.

The reason is that video engages multiple senses: sight and hearing. We are far more likely to form permanent memories when an experience engages more than one sense at a time. Video is also better at evoking emotions than text alone—and emotions, like senses, are closely tied to memory.

Even without its advantages around memorability, video tops any other form of marketing (except perhaps face-to-face interactions) when it comes to building authentic relationships. Through video, your community can see you, hear you, and feel you. They can get to know your expressions, your body language, and your mannerisms. Since more than 80 percent of communication is nonverbal, video adds a key layer to the "know, like, trust" equation.

We'll get into the specifics of how to use video to Legendeer your marketing in Part II. For now, understand that it is integral to this directive for all the reasons we've explored in this chapter. If you're not already using it in your business, it's time to start.

CHAPTER FOUR
DON'T BE SELFISH

It's Not About You

CONTENT MARKETING wasn't invented by social media gurus. It wasn't invented by *Mad Men*-type advertising execs in the 1950s. It wasn't invented by department stores or turn-of-the-century snake oil salesmen pushing laudanum as a tonic for anxious mothers.

No, content marketing is far older than that. It's my belief that it originated somewhere around the time the printing press was invented, but the first known example we have comes from none other than Benjamin Franklin.

You see, Franklin owned a printing company in Philadelphia that he wanted to promote. He also had a vision for making helpful information like astrological data, weather predictions, recipes, and life advice available to the average person. So, in 1733, he invented a character named Richard Saunders and wrote a magazine-like almanac in his voice. Then, he printed, published, and distributed it through his company.

Poor Richard's Almanack became a bestseller in its own right, selling nearly 10,000 copies a year until Franklin ceased publication in 1759, which, when you consider that the entire population of the American colonies at that time was under 1 million people, is nothing short of astounding.

What makes *Poor Richard's Almanack* both a showpiece of content marketing and an inspiration for Legendeering isn't how well it sold, but rather the intention with which it was created. In Franklin's own words, *"I endeavoured to make it both entertaining and useful, and it accordingly came to be in such demand that I reaped considerable profit from it ..."*

While one intention around creating the almanac may have been to grow his printing business, Franklin didn't design his work with sales as his primary goal. Instead, he asked, "How can I use my skills to fill a clear need for my community?" You see, at the time, books were rare and expensive, and only successful people could afford them. *Poor Richard's Almanack* provided key information for a large chunk of the colonial population as well as entertaining stories, puzzles, and advice they couldn't find anywhere else. This information came with no strings attached; consumers didn't need to purchase printing services to benefit from what Franklin had produced. In essence, he was "buying dinner" for more than 1 percent of the American colonial population every year. A percentage of that community then reciprocated by supporting his business, because that's what humans do.

Most of what we know as "content marketing" today misses this vital point. Instead of, "Here's something you need—enjoy!" it's more like, "Here's a cool story—but if you want the ending, you need to buy my stuff." Just because you're producing content doesn't mean you're doing content marketing.

The Content Marketing Institute defines content marketing this way:

> *Content marketing is a strategic marketing approach focused on creating and distributing valuable, relevant, and consistent content to attract and retain a clearly defined audience—and, ultimately, to drive profitable customer action.*

However, this definition misses one critically important piece.

The number-one factor in successful content marketing is that *it is not directly related to your products and services*. There are no strings attached. That doesn't mean there can't be a paywall—after all, people had to buy *Poor Richard's Almanack* to get the content—but that transaction, from the viewpoint of the customer, was all about *what they were getting*, not what Richard Saunders (aka Ben Franklin) was receiving.

Think about the last concert ticket you bought. When you entered your credit card information, you were probably thinking about how much fun you would have, or how close to the band you'd get, or maybe that you'd been wanting to hear the opening act but hadn't had a chance yet. Maybe you considered that the band would make money from your purchase—but that was likely a passing thought. From the time you heard about the concert to the moment you left the venue, the experience was *all about you*. And whether you paid $30 or $300 (or more) for your tickets, you probably considered it a bargain for the quality of your experience.

Know what you didn't think about? That the venue made money. That the tour managers made money. That the record labels made money. That the bartenders made money. (Okay, if you've ever tended bar, you might have considered that for a hot second.) Long story short, no one buys a concert ticket because the sound engineers are awesome, or because they want to support the roadies. Trying to sell tickets that way wouldn't work.

If Benjamin Franklin had tried to sell his services by waxing poetic about the quality of his paper, the depth of tone of his ink, the speed of his presses, or how amazing it was for him to be a rich man in

Philadelphia, would anyone have cared? Probably not. Instead, he created an offer that gave more value to the end user than the money he was charging for it.

So, why do so many people and businesses try to make their marketing all about *them*?

It's Not About You. It's About Them

When we're taught how to market our products and services, particularly in the online space, it's focused on us: how we're showing up, what we're saying (or not saying), and what we're selling (or not selling).

I'm here to tell you, no one cares about that stuff.

Or, more accurately, they won't care about that stuff *until* you've demonstrated that you can offer value to them in a way that makes their lives better.

Consider the following example.

In 1900, the auto industry was still in its infancy. Only a select few were able to afford cars, and the "driving experience" was a thrilling new adventure for many. The Michelin brothers, Édouard and André, owners of a French tire manufacturing company, decided to create a travel guide for drivers to make these excursions more fun, safe, and exciting. At first, the guide contained only basic information about how to change a tire, listings for mechanics along well-known routes, and other stuff you'd expect from a tire company.

Then, one day, André visited one of their local tire vendors and saw the latest round of the *Michelin*

Guide being used to prop up a workbench. Obviously, people were not receiving value from what was being published.

André and his brother started asking, "What other information is valuable to motorists?" This being France, the first thing that came to mind was food.

The guide was expanded to include information about restaurants. Immediately, the publication surged in popularity. Soon, the Michelin brothers hired inspectors to go and review each restaurant based on a specific set of criteria. This led to the famous "star system" that, today, is one of the most coveted rankings in the restaurant world.

The Michelin brothers, like Ben Franklin, tapped into the truth at the heart of Legendeering Directive #3: "It's not about you. It's about them." They were selling tires, not food—and yet, meeting this need in their target market using a clean, no-strings-attached approach catapulted them to the top of their industry, where they have stayed for more than 120 years. In fact, their content marketing venture was so successful that, like Franklin's almanac, it became its own revenue stream and its own brand—to the point where most people recognize the Michelin name as a standard in the food industry, not as a tire company.

If the Michelin brothers were starting out today, they might have produced a video series where their inspectors visited each restaurant, tasted the food, and ranked it accordingly. I like to think that it would have been every bit as successful.

This type of approach, regardless of format, is a long game. It's serve, serve, and serve some more—because it's not about you. It's about them. So, when you're planning your next sales funnel, email sequence, video series, or blog post, ask yourself ...

"Who is this really about—me or them?"

My friend, Geraldine Laybourne, former President of Nickelodeon and co-founder of Oxygen Media, agrees with this "serve first, sell second" approach. In a recent conversation, she told me, "I was on a plane flying home from a business trip. Oprah Winfrey, me, and Marcy Carsey were on the cover of *Forbes* announcing Oxygen—which immediately focused the microscope. There was a young man sitting next to me, and I noticed that he was reading over my shoulder.

"'I see that you're working with these powerful people,' he said to me. 'What is the quickest way to get rich?'

"At this point, we're flying over Nevada. I can see the lights of the Las Vegas strip thirty thousand feet below us. And I said, 'I am so sorry to tell you this, but the fact that you're asking me that question means that you'll never be rich. Oprah did not set out to get rich. Marcy Carsey did not set out to get rich. I did not set out to get rich. We all had a value that we brought to the space, and we wanted to open up a dialogue with an audience. If we had focused on getting rich, we would never have gotten to where we are.'"

WHO ARE YOU TALKING TO?

If you're having a hard time deciding what your version of the *Michelin Guide* or *Poor Richard's Almanack* could be, don't worry. I've got you covered.

Since most of us don't intuitively approach our marketing from the standpoint of "It's about them," it's hard to know what questions to ask. After all, we've been told for so long that we need to talk about our offers, communicate our value, sell our results and outcomes, etc. But when you look beneath the surface, that stuff is all about us. That's why most marketing efforts fall flat.

Your content marketing should *intentionally* have nothing to do with what, why, when, or where you're selling.

You'll notice that I left the "who" out of that statement. Because the "who"—meaning, your ideal community—is still the same, and your marketing should have everything to do with them.

If your business is operating with any degree of success, you should have some idea of who your community is. However, I'd like to invite you to step away from what you know and look at this group of people with fresh eyes.

Your ideal community is comprised of three groups:

- Existing customers—people who have already bought your stuff.

- Potential customers—people who will buy your stuff in the future.

- Potential referral partners —people who will advocate for your business even if they never buy from you.

(That last group is one that few businesses pay attention to—but remember, it's not about you. It's about them.)

Your work is to identify the profiles of the people in the three groups above and use that information to grow a community around your brand. Who do you want to be a part of your community? Who do you derive value from? Who do you admire? Who do you want to advocate for?

(Notice I didn't ask, "Who do *you* want to buy your stuff?" That's secondary.)

Choose people you actually want to be around, hang out with, and talk to—because if you don't interact with them, it's not a community, it's an audience. When in doubt, always choose community over audience.

This next bit may seem tangential, but I promise you it's not.

I often ask my business clients, "Who was your first customer?" Chances are, it wasn't some random person off the street. It was someone who knew, liked, and trusted them, and who they were excited to do a great job for. When retailers throw grand opening parties, who shows up first? Friends, family, and neighbors—aka, community. When a new restaurant opens, who writes the first reviews? You guessed it: friends, family, and neighbors. There are relationships at play that go deeper than transactions.

People who favor audience over community often cite things like "aspirational identity," "exclusivity," and "luxury." They *want* the brand to feel out of reach. Candidly, I think that's bullshit. It's form over function, like every other standard ad model, and that's not a sustainable approach to running a business. You can already see the decline of audience-based "influencer" marketing; at some point, people get tired of keeping up with the Joneses and move on. Of course, it's possible to build a lasting luxury brand—just look at Chanel, Lancôme, Armani, and others—but you don't do that by keeping people out. You do that by inviting *the right people* in.

One of the best examples of the community approach (as opposed to the audience approach) is what we're currently seeing in podcast advertising. The advertiser sends pre-written copy to the podcaster, who then completely changes it to fit their own voice, flavor, and tone. It's very common for the host to make jokes, make comparisons, and generally say things that would have traditional ad execs losing their minds—but in the end, it feels authentic, as though the host genuinely knows, likes, and trusts the products they're endorsing. And while traditional ad spots are only thirty to sixty seconds long, podcast ads hold listeners' attention for two to three minutes or more.

All this is to say that, to build a legendary brand, you need to focus on community over audience, and then populate that community with people who share your values and with whom you actually want to interact—even if a portion of them will never actually buy your stuff.

Now, back to those three groups within your community.

The first two groups are pretty easy to identify. They're the ones who need, want, and will buy your product or service, now or at some point in the future. For my client Lyn, a Realtor in New York City, those are people looking to buy homes in NYC now or in the near future. Simple enough.

But the third group? That's where things get fun.

What about the people who already live in New York and are curious about the history of the neighborhoods where they currently live? What about the people who live upstate, but have friends and colleagues who want to move to the city—and who could refer those people to Lyn when they are ready to engage a Realtor?

When we Legendeered Lyn's content strategy, we didn't focus on real estate, glamorous Upper West Side homes, or the logistics of moving to New York—even though all of those are key aspects of her work. Instead, we focused on her passion for green spaces in NYC. Her content plan showcases the various neighborhood parks that exist in the city, the stories of how those parks came to be, and how the community benefits from each of them. By highlighting the neighborhoods she works in, without any reference to her work as a Realtor, she's able to give people a taste of what it's like to live in New York while simultaneously supporting the green space projects she's passionate about.

Remember, the first step is always to make people give a shit.

The Domino's Effect

If everything we've reviewed in this chapter hasn't persuaded you to make your marketing about your customers, let's talk about how this approach saved Domino's Pizza.

Domino's was founded in Michigan in the 1960s and went on to become a successful national franchise. When the company went public in 2004, they were enjoying annual revenues of about $1.5 billion. However, over the next six years, that revenue deflated to about $1.4 billion in 2010. Needless to say, executives and shareholders were confused.

During this time, Twitter was also becoming the primary platform through which giant companies like Domino's could receive feedback directly from customers. After looking at the online chatter, they realized that one of the primary things hurting sales was the pizza itself. People didn't like it. It tasted like cardboard. In fact, the pizza was so bad that, in a national taste test, it came in dead last among all American national chains—tied with Chuck E.

Cheese, which, as you know, is not even a pizza chain, but rather an indoor playground facility that also happens to serve pizza.

Things were looking bad for Domino's. So, they decided that, in order to deliver for their customers (pun intended), they had to fix their pizza. But first, they did something that no other major national corporation had ever done before: they created a video holding themselves accountable to their fans.

In this video—which was so novel that it actually spawned the term "radical authenticity"—Domino's executives, marketers, and chefs aired all of their dirty laundry. They shared that they were devastated that their mission to make delicious, affordable pizza had gone off the rails, and promised to fix the issues.

If you'll forgive me another pun, that video, titled "Domino's Pizza Turnaround," was the first "domino" to fall in Domino's new, customer-focused marketing strategy. While they made several more good videos after their initial release, most analysts credit that single video with empowering the company's growth from $1.4 billion in 2010 to $3.5 billion in 2019, with 5,000 stores added globally.

Of course, the other piece of this comeback story is the pizza itself. After their vulnerable, authentic sharing in the "Pizza Turnaround" video, Domino's execs did, in fact, fix their pizza. It now ranks much higher in national taste tests. They listened to their customers and gave them exactly what they asked for, rather than simply doing what was best or easiest for themselves.

The result—because of the Law of Reciprocity—was a level of customer excitement and loyalty that carried the company through ten years of exponential growth.

So, yes, this stuff works.

But there are two more takeaways I'd like to highlight.

First, the "Pizza Turnaround" campaign would never have been possible without video. No press release or radio interview could have accurately conveyed the level of concern, contrition, and commitment that the video captured. Customers met and got to know the Domino's leadership team, including the President, CMO, and head chefs, all of whom appeared genuine in their desire to do better. People gave them a second chance because they connected with them on a human level.

Second, that video provided a ton of opportunity for major media coverage. The video was so revolutionary that it made headlines all over the country. News organizations picked it up and ran with it. Then, when Domino's started releasing new recipes, those same news outlets started doing live taste tests to confirm that the pizza really *was* better than before. The whole thing got so out of control that it sparked a "pizza war" between the big players in the industry. Companies like Pizza Hut, Papa John's, and others were adding new menu items, tweaking their own recipes, and generally scrambling to keep up with the public's rekindled enthusiasm for good pizza.

The coolest part? In that whole "Pizza Turnaround" campaign, *not once* did Domino's actually try to sell anyone their pizza—and yet, people couldn't wait to get in line.

That's the power of leading with value.

The Art of Awareness

A lot of people are confused about the difference between marketing and sales. In fact, many of the strategies that get passed off as "marketing" in the online space are actually sales strategies, which is why they feel so gross and misaligned.

It's also why true content marketing—the kind I center in Legendeering—can feel so counterintuitive to those who have been steeped in modern "marketing" tactics.

So, let's go there.

Marketing is the art and practice of creating an awareness of your brand and its values within your chosen community. In the Legendeering strategy, we use long-form episodic video content to create this awareness while delivering value with no strings attached.

Sales, on the other hand, is the art and practice of turning interested parties into buyers.

ROI, details, program components, product specs, and outcomes are all *sales information*. They are of value to those who are already interested in buying your stuff. However, they have no place in marketing, and may actually repel people who could become interested parties later. Even those who don't sell out-right in their marketing make this mistake. All those posts about how many years you've been in business, how many clients you have, what tools you use, how much you charge, what awards you've won ... imagining being on the receiving end of all that from a company you've never heard of before. That info should absolutely be available on your website or further down in your sales funnel, but it should never be a first touch. Why? For the same reason you wouldn't walk up to someone on the street and say, "Buy my awesome widget."

Leading with sales doesn't build relationships. So, you can imagine why I get frustrated when people ask, "What's the ROI on Legendeered video content?"

Unless your content has a direct link to buy, you cannot calculate its ROI. You can *guess* how much your Legendeered content has helped your revenue overall (as we learned in the Introduction, businesses that use video experience an average of 49 percent higher revenue growth), but you can't pin a number on it, any more than you can put a price tag on your closest friendships. It's not about how your relationships pay out today, or tomorrow. It's about how they will bring value to both of you over the course of a lifetime.

Many marketers will try to measure the ROI on their marketing by calculating brand recognition, perceived value, and other intangibles. "We have a survey," they'll say, "in which we ask potential customers where they first heard of us." Newsflash: people can't remember their own wedding anniversaries or their spouses' birthdays—and they *care* about those. They *may* remember that they clicked on a Facebook ad to get to your website (and your survey) because it happened thirty seconds ago. But chances are, if they clicked on an ad, it's not the first time they've been exposed to your brand. Somewhere, in some way, they were exposed to a piece (or multiple pieces) of marketing that made them feel good about their decision to click on your ad.

In short, your marketing is not interchangeable with, nor is it a replacement for, your sales strategy. They both play a vital role, but they don't do the same things.

CHAPTER FIVE

IRONMAN, GALAXY WARS, AND OTHER TALES

Why We All Love a Good Story

IN MARCH OF 2022, I set a goal to complete my second Ironman race in late August at Mont-Tremblant in Quebec. I knew this goal would push me to the max, so I decided to Legendeer this journey by sharing one short video for every day of my training. This, I reasoned, would have the effect of not only building my personal portfolio of Legendeered content but also hold me accountable to the training process.

Things were going well for a little while. I talked about my exercise process, my mental process, and my nutrition. Then, on day twelve, things took a hard left turn.

That day, my ride had a bunch of sprint intervals. On the first set, my bike chain slipped, but I was in the saddle, so it wasn't a big deal. During the second set of intervals, I was out of the saddle, pushing really hard. The chain slipped again—and over the handlebars I went.

I landed on the left side of my face, knocked myself out, and broke my collarbone in three places. The rest of the day was spent in the emergency room. Thank God I had my helmet on, or I likely wouldn't be here to write this chapter.

My vlog for day twelve featured me, in a sling, with some truly gorgeous road rash on my face, recounting the incident with my eyes still a bit glazed from the concussion. It would have been easy for me to skip my video that day, but I didn't.

Someone asked me in the comments, "Is this the end of your training then?"

My response: "Heck, no. This just got interesting!"

The advice of the doctors was to rest, heal, and try again next year. I would need surgery to reset my collarbone, and the recovery period was predicted to be three to four months long. But I wasn't going to let a broken bone stop me. I knew this setback wasn't the end of the story.

On day thirteen, my training was reduced from a six-mile run to walking on my treadmill at a moderate pace (so as not to jostle my shoulder)—but I still trained. And I still made my video.

When I tell this story at speaking engagements, I

have a slide that shows the X-ray of my collarbone neatly snapped in three places. (Cue the pained cringe from the audience.) After I share my decision to continue training in the face of adversity—with the evidence of my injury on full display—I ask the audience, "Who's rooting for me to succeed and finish this race?"

Every hand in the room goes up. Every time.

The reason for this isn't the intensity of my story, because it's not actually that intense. People get hurt all the time, and to far worse degrees than I was. No, the reason that audiences consistently root for me to succeed is that, as humans, we are socially—and maybe even genetically—programmed to do so.

We love an underdog. We love a good comeback. We love witnessing triumph over any kind of adversity—physical, emotional, or spiritual.

But, most of all, we love a good story.

We Are Wired for Story

As you may recall from our discussion in Chapter One, story is one of the most powerful tools in our evolution as a species. That's why we use it so often and so naturally, and why it's central to the Legendeering strategy.

If you look at story as a teaching medium, you'll see examples going back into antiquity. Some of these stories are hundreds, even thousands, of years old. Epics, fairy tales, fables, and even children's songs are packed full of moral and practical lessons about how to do basic survival tasks, when natural phenomena tend to happen, how to treat other people, and how to stay safe in times of danger. (Look up the meaning of "Ring Around the Rosie." It's a kid-friendly set of instructions for avoiding the bubonic plague.)

Of particular significance is the framework of the Hero's Journey. This story format has been used, implicitly or explicitly, in every beloved tale in history—from *The Iliad* and *The Odyssey*, *The Mahabharata*, (in particular in the *Bhagavad Gita*, which is contained within that epic), and the Biblical tale of Moses, to *Star Wars*, *The Matrix*, and *Harry Potter*. Identified by story and mythology expert Joseph Campbell and expounded in his popular book, *The Hero with a Thousand Faces*, the Hero's Journey has three clear parts: the Separation, in which the hero leaves their "ordinary" life and sets out on a journey; the Initiation, in which the hero meets their mentors and has epic adventures; and the Return, in which the hero returns victorious but irrevocably changed.

These three parts are further broken out into twelve steps:

Part 1: The Separation

1. **The Ordinary World.** The hero is shown living a normal life (or, what passes for "normal" for the hero at that time).

2. **The Call to Adventure.** The hero is called forward into action by forces internal or external.

3. **The Refusal of the Call.** The hero hesitates or refuses to act because of fear, limitations, or other factors.

4. **Meeting the Mentor.** The hero meets a teacher or guide (or identifies with an internal higher expression of self).

Part 2: The Initiation

5. **Crossing the Threshold.** The choice that means there's no going back.

6. **Trials, Allies, and Enemies.** Adventures along the way to the ultimate goal.

7. **Approach to the Innermost Cave.** The fears, self-doubts, challenges, and preparations as the hero prepares to face the final challenge.

8. **The Supreme Ordeal.** The final challenge standing between the hero and their goal.

9. **Reward.** The moment when the prize is won.

Part 3: The Return

10. **The Road Back.** Resolving any lingering challenges, wrapping up loose ends.

11. **Resurrection.** The hero steps fully into this new version/expression of themselves and claims their new powers/skills/position.

12. **Return with the Elixir.** The hero is back where they started, but everything is different.

Out of the Hero's Journey, which Campbell dubbed "the Monomyth," have grown numerous other sub-frameworks that may be familiar, such as the "Rags to Riches" journey, the "Once Upon a Time" journey, the "Big Idea" journey, the "Tempestuous Romance" journey, and many more. Yes, some modern stories don't fit precisely into the three-part structure of the Hero's Journey—but among the stories that are the most popular, compelling, and memorable, the Monomyth framework is almost universal.

The story I tell audiences about my Ironman training is a short and sweet example of the Hero's Journey. I started off "ordinary," meaning that I wasn't yet capable of taking on a physical challenge of this magnitude. I set off on an adventure (my training). I had a setback, but I persevered and crossed the threshold (of my own commitment) when I could have turned back. Now, all that is left is for me to bring in allies (which, in this case, are actually the audience), and keep pushing for the win.

At the time of this writing, I am over 120 days into my training, and three weeks away from that Ironman trial. My Supreme Ordeal is yet to come—but I know I'll get through it, and I know I'll come home forever changed by this experience. More, my community of viewers will be right there with me to witness the whole thing—and, hopefully, learn something about their own capacity for achievement at the same time.

STORY > INFORMATION

If I were to simply say to the groups I present to, "I'm doing an Ironman," it wouldn't do nearly as much to enroll people in my story as the full Hero's Journey story. Why? Because information alone isn't interesting to people.

Story is the best learning tool we have as humans because information is only interesting, memorable, and useful if we can contextualize it in the framework of our own lives. Story, particularly the emotional components of story, helps us do that in a way that's also fun and engaging. When you're rooting for the hero, you care about the outcome. You're invested. And what's interesting and relevant to the hero becomes interesting and relevant to you.

You can leverage this age-old framework in nearly infinite ways. In the Legendeering framework, it will be among your greatest assets. However, with so many possible story subjects, it can be easy to get a bit lost and confused.

When considering what stories you want to tell, keep these three things in mind:

1. What is the story?
2. What are you trying to teach or demonstrate to your audience through this story (aka, what's the angle)?
3. How is this story about them (your viewers), rather than about you?

Particularly in the context of building a community around your brand, angle is everything. Think about the original *Star Wars* movies. If the story had been about space wars and light sabers alone, it wouldn't have been very relatable. How could we possibly find common ground with a tiny green Jedi? But those details of time, place, and character were simply accessories to the superbly relatable human story of young leaders coming into their destiny and facing critical choices upon which their entire future (and that of the galaxy) would hinge. Everyone knows what it's like to be scared of the future and feel like your choices could make or break the rest of your life. Everyone knows what it's like to be in over your head.

When you use story to tap into universal human themes like love, belonging, adventure, adversity, sadness, and hope, you will enroll your audience regardless of the subjects you choose.

STORIES AND SALES DON'T MIX

There's a trend, on social media in particular but also in print media, where people are tacking sales pitches onto the end of their stories. Content creators will create beautiful posts or videos about an epic journey in their lives, complete with all the high and low points inherent to the Hero's Journey. They'll enroll viewers emotionally and intellectually by speaking to the common elements of their experience, make them care, teach them something important, bring it all to a peak, and then ...

They slap you across the face with a sales pitch.

"If this resonates with you, buy my widget!"

What felt like genuine connection is, with a few sentences and a URL, revealed to be entirely transactional. The more emotionally invested your readers have become across the telling of your tale, the more dissonant this tactic will feel, and the more they will resent you for it. Despite initial appearances, you weren't using your story to teach, connect, and convey information, as we humans are naturally inclined to do. Instead, you were using it to manipulate people into taking an action that benefits you—and your viewers know it. From now on, they'll be thinking, "This person doesn't really care about me. They only want my money."

Honestly, it's like sending a birthday card and gift to a friend, and then signing the card like this: *I hope you like your gift! Here's my mailing address so you can give me a gift of the same caliber on my birthday, which, as you'll recall, is on July 1. Hope you enjoy your day! PS: I also expect a thank you note within two weeks, or I'll assume you didn't appreciate the deep thought and iteration that went into this gift I'm sending.*

Just send the damn card.

Just give the damn gift.

Just *tell the damn story.*

Mainstream marketing gurus encourage this "sales in every post" approach because they know that story primes the reader emotionally to buy. "You need a call to action (CTA) in every post," they'll say, "otherwise people won't know what you do or how to find you!"

As you've guessed, I disagree. Sales only occur *after* trust has been built through giving without expectation (Directive #1), being radically authentic (Directive #2), and remembering that it's not about you, it's about them (Directive #3). So, stop attaching strings to everything. When you use story as a connection and teaching tool in your marketing, remember these directives. Then, when you do make a (highly valuable, strategic, and compelling) sales invitation, people will be excited to receive it.

With true connection as a baseline, sales are not only natural, but easy.

What Stories Should You Tell?

In addition to leading with value, being relentlessly authentic, and putting your customers first (the first three directives), Legendeered content always starts with story, then follows up with facts. If you're not telling a compelling story, no one will give a shit about your information—even if it's great information. And, as we've learned, in order for people to give a shit about your products, you have to make them give a shit about *you*—and the most effective way to do that is to prove you give a shit about *them*.

People don't care how much you know, until they know how much you care about them. That's why Directive #4 of Legendeering is: "Start with Story, Follow Up with Facts."

But ... what stories should you tell, and how?

Since you're not using story as a sales vehicle, you'll have a *lot* of room to play with storytelling in your content. In fact, there are *endless* possibilities for what you talk about, and where, and with whom. The only limit is your imagination.

That said, a wide-open field isn't super helpful when it comes to choosing a story for that first video! To help you narrow it down, I want to share an adaptation of the Hero's Journey structure that's ubiquitous in episodic television: the Four-Act Structure.

Any thirty-minute television show you watch follows this structure. It's basically the Hero's Journey in four acts instead of three. Those acts are:

- **Act I: Laying the Foundation.** This is where we get to know the setting and main characters—meaning, you or the people from your organization who are starring in the video.

- **Act II: The Action.** This is where we meet the secondary characters—the people you are interviewing, or who are helping you tell the story. These could be your clients, your staff, or anyone relevant to the story you've chosen to tell. This is also where the inciting event—aka, "crossing the threshold"—happens and begins to move the story forward.

- **Act III: The Climax.** This is where the big
  tension happens. Will they or won't they?
  Will our hero triumph? What will happen
  next?

- **Act IV: The Resolution.** This is the "Return"
  in the Hero's Journey, the place where con-
  flict is resolved and the story is wrapped up
  in a tidy bow.

If you can map the story you want to tell to that
structure, it will most likely play well for your audience, even if the production is as simple as you talking
into your iPhone.

Once you know that your story idea can be mapped
to the Four-Act Structure, ask the following helpful
questions:

- **Does your story take the audience on a
  journey?** When I'm producing videos, I
  always think about taking the audience on
  a roller coaster ride. You get on the roller
  coaster, you do that slow climb up to the
  peak (That's Act I: Building the Foundation),
  then you hit the first big drop (Act II: The
  Action). Then, there's a bunch of twists and
  turns, maybe a loop, your stomach drops
  out, you're not sure if you're having fun or
  you're scared (Act III: The Climax)—and
  then, just when you think you're going to
  puke, you're pulling back into the station

(Act IV: The Resolution) and you leave with a smile on your face. When you can wrap excitement, anticipation, nervousness, confusion, and real caring into a story, then wrap it all up in a hopeful bow, your audience will keep coming back for more.

- **Is your idea repeatable?** Can this same story structure be expressed in multiple ways across multiple episodes so your content feels congruent?

- **Is this time and cost efficient?** Unless you have a bottomless budget, your story idea shouldn't require you to fly to Iceland with a film crew, buy expensive equipment, or spend multiple days shooting a single video. Ideally, you should be able to film multiple story episodes in one day. (More on that in the Production section in Part II.)

- **Are you making people's lives better?** Once the audience watches your content, will their lives be improved in some way? Have you educated them, made them laugh, made them cry, or made them care? Story for story's sake is nice; story that inspires change is brilliant.

I know that this all seems really complex—but trust me, it's not. In fact, the way you naturally tell stories likely fits perfectly into this model. Just punch it up a bit, and you'll be off to the races (maybe even literally).

However, there's one more criterion I want to present before you start writing video frameworks: whatever content you choose to create for your audience, *you* have to be excited about it. Like, really excited. That kind of enthusiasm is catchy as hell, and it can't be faked.

Remember Lyn, the Realtor from New York I introduced you to in Chapter Four? Her strategy to focus on green spaces was actually not the first one we landed on. Initially, to create her Legendeered content, we planned to interview key people in the neighborhoods in which she was selling high-end real estate—people like restaurant owners, vendors, doormen, and other community mainstays.

However, after sitting with it, Lyn confessed, "I'm not excited about this."

That was enough for us to toss out the whole strategy. You can't fake excitement, especially if the goal is to be relentlessly authentic. And so, I asked, "What does get you excited? What are your favorite parts of the neighborhoods?"

Instantly, Lyn shared her passion for green spaces and parks. These little oases of nature in the concrete jungle are essential to the wellbeing of the city and its residents. And, because of her passion for preserving them, Lyn knew *everyone* in that sphere—from the students who led the charge to protect Morningside Park from development, to the head of the Carl Schurz Park Conservancy who helped save the park that is home to Gracie Mansion, to the couple who have run a volunteer park clean-up initiative for thirty years and have no intention of retiring, to the NYC Parks Supervisor whom everyone knows by name.

I suggested, "What if we did a series on the parks in the neighborhoods you sell in? We can tell stories about their creation, their maintenance, their revitalization, and the magic that happens there."

I saw the spark come back to Lyn's eyes. We'd hit on *the thing*.

From there, it was easy to create a repeatable format using the Four-Act Structure. There are literally endless opportunities within this framework to tell compelling stories—and Lyn's friends within the parks community are beyond excited to share their time and expertise. And why wouldn't they be? She's *making it about them!*

This angle was perfect for Lyn because it met all of the criteria mentioned above. The stories we wanted to tell were adaptable to the Four-Act Structure and took the audience on a journey. The idea was repeatable. Since Lyn already knew many of the key players, it was time and cost efficient. And, most importantly, each story had the potential to make viewers' lives better—whether they were planning to move to New York City or not.

There are as many ways to create content as there are businesses. In addition to personal stories from your own life and business, you have many assets around you to draw from—including your current customers, your employees, your neighbors, your friends, the businesses who peripherally benefit from your services, and so much more. Another client of mine who runs an insurance agency recently decided to do a content series on the multiple charities to which his agency donates on a monthly basis. By featuring the charities, he demonstrates his values around social responsibility and giving back to the community without saying a word about his products. Yet, who do you think his philanthropically-aligned community members will choose when they need a new homeowner's policy? It's a no-brainer.

Inevitably, when I do this work with clients, there comes a moment when a particular content idea makes them light up. "Yes!" they say. "That's who I am!" Remember, relentless authenticity builds trust. Yes, this content is meant to serve—but it also needs to represent your values. This should be as exciting for you as it is for your community. Think of it as your version of the *Michelin Guide*.

If you're still not sure what your *"Michelin Guide"* is, or how to provide value to your community through value-driven content, just look at your calendar! What are you involved in, outside of your products and services, that you are passionate about? Civic organizations? Business organizations? Charities? Ironman triathlons?

Above all, remember: It's not about you. It's about them. Your stories will land far more powerfully if you tell them for your audience, rather than for yourself.

CHAPTER SIX

DON'T BURN THE HOUSE DOWN

A Lesson in Consistency

WHEN I WAS about ten years old, my parents decided it was time to let me stay home alone.

This was, of course, super exciting for me. Up until that point, I'd often been left in the care of my older sister, which was less fun for her than it was for me. It felt like a huge milestone to be completely on my own—and since this milestone event took place years before everyone and their kid had a smartphone, I would only have myself to rely on.

Mom and Dad laid down the usual rules: don't play with matches, don't kill yourself doing dumb stunts, and don't open the door for anyone you don't know. I nodded along eagerly. "Yup. Don't start fires. Don't die. Got it, Ma."

Then, the big day came. "Tom, we're going to the grocery store. We'll be gone about an hour. Can we trust you to do as we've asked?"

They could. That first trial was uneventful. I even exceeded expectations by picking up after myself. The next time they left me alone, it was for two hours. Then, it was for half a day. And, by the time I was twelve, my parents knew they could trust me to take care of myself for a full day. With each episode of independence, I grew more and more sure of myself, and, unexpectedly, began to look for other ways to prove to my parents that I was trustworthy and mature.

And ... that's it.

If you were waiting for a "but, then ..." type of story, I'm sorry to disappoint. Nothing bad ever happened while I was home alone. In fact, it was pretty boring most of the time.

So, why should you care about my childhood non-adventures? Because this is a story about *consistency* and *expectations*, and you'll need to understand both to master Legendeering Directive #5: "Consistency is Key."

My parents set clear expectations for me in the form of ground rules, and I exceeded them. As they learned that they could trust me, they gave me more autonomy. By being trustworthy consistently, I earned the right to ask for more time home alone and more of

Chapter Six: Don't Burn the House Down | 91

the grown-up responsibilities I wanted. It was a natural progression.

The exact same concept applies to your marketing. You can lead with value, give without expectations, be relentlessly authentic, make it all about your community, and tell all the best stories—and *none of it will matter if you don't show up consistently.*

Consistency + Meeting Expectations = Trust

The reason consistency matters is the same reason that relentless authenticity matters: because it creates trust.

As a child, I was consistent when it came to being safe while home alone. After the tenth time I didn't sever an artery or torch the kitchen while my parents were out, they started to relax and feel like they could count on me to do the right thing. That trust extended beyond the container of "home alone" into other areas of our family life, like using power tools with my dad and, when I was old enough, driving the family car. As a teenager, I made some questionable decisions and was a bit less consistent—but never enough to shatter that foundation of trust. I had leeway to mess up a little because I'd been so consistent for so long.

Now, imagine that I had done really great during my first hour home alone, but the second time my parents left me at home, I decided to dance naked in the front yard, or build a pair of wings out of blankets and broomsticks so I could jump off the roof. Then, the third time, I did okay again—but the time after that, I threw a raging party and let my friends eat all the food my mom had cooked for the week. Do you think the results (meaning, my parents trusting me and offering me more autonomy) would have been remotely the same? Not a chance.

When people engage with your brand, they are essentially doing those first "home alone" tests. If you consistently meet or exceed expectations, they will begin to trust you. When trust is established, reciprocity feels natural and easy. They'll begin to lean in, to expect you to show up in the ways you've established as "normal" for you and your brand. And when they know they can count on you to show up consistently with your content, especially when (on the surface) there's nothing in it for you except service, they will feel more comfortable trusting you with their business and their friends' business.

LEGENDEERED CONTENT IS CONSISTENT

In Chapter Five, we learned how to format a powerful story and use it to create authentic, community-focused episodic content. You may have gathered from that discussion that *episodic* content is foundational to Legendeering because it helps you tell good stories in a repeatable format. This is true.

However, episodic content also creates *consistency*

and sets clear *expectations*, which in turn fosters trust. When you format your content this way, your community knows exactly what to expect and when to expect it, and so feel relief from their fear of the unknown.

"Really?" you may be thinking. "Fear of the unknown is *actually* a thing when it comes to video content?"

You bet it is. When people know what they're getting, they feel comforted. Held. Secure. And, surprisingly, it doesn't appear to diminish their interest levels; rather, it elevates them.

Consider the long-running television show *Law & Order (duh-dun)*. Chances are, if you watch any network television at all, you've seen an episode of this show. The original *Law & Order* is, at the time of this writing, in its twenty-first season, having recently been revived after an eleven-year hiatus. The show also spawned six spin-offs (with a seventh currently in the works); the most popular of those, *Law & Order: Special Victims Unit*, is the longest-running prime-time live-action series in the history of American television, with over 515 episodes.

Why do people love this show so much? Sure, it's dramatic. It's informative. It's interesting. But most of all, it's *consistent*. Each episode starts at a crime scene and follows the ensuing investigation. Then, there's an arrest, and a suspect is charged. The case goes to the prosecutor's office, and then to court, where there's a climactic moment. Finally, the show wraps up with a clear conclusion—a verdict, a plea deal, or some other resolution. The bad guy is always caught, and the law always triumphs, even if that triumph is messy and comes at a cost to the "good guys."

Does this feel familiar? Maybe it reminds you of the Four-Act Structure. Do you see how this same formula plays out consistently, predictably, and successfully across literally thousands of episodes and multiple spin-offs?

When you're flipping through television channels looking for something to watch, and you see a *Law & Order* title come up, you know exactly what you're going to get. You know what kind of story and action to expect, what themes might be in play, and how it will end. It's as comforting and familiar as sinking into the warm embrace of your favorite chair.

If you're not a *Law & Order* fan, I challenge you to apply this logic to whatever television show you're currently bingeing. Sitcoms, home renovation shows, and kids' series are great places to start. Remember Steve Irwin, star of *The Crocodile Hunter*? That show inspired millions of kids with predictably formatted (but still "wicked exciting") episodic content. Same with *Mister Rogers' Neighborhood* and more recent YouTube shows like *Blippi* or Coyote Peterson's *Brave Wilderness*.

(Note: Today, many popular streaming "TV" series follow longer arcs and are more like ten-hour movies than episodic shows. They still follow the same rules of storytelling and employ a structure similar to the Four-Act Structure, but that structure may be harder to see in the larger story arc. So, I'd suggest you don't model your own content after *Game of Thrones* or *Outlander.* There's a reason George R.R. Martin and Diana Gabaldon take ten years to write every book.)

Just like the most successful episodic television shows, your Legendeered content should tell engaging stories consistently, according to a repeatable and predictable formula that doesn't change drastically in focus across episodes. Your formula can look however you want, as long as it takes viewers on a journey. However, if you change it up with every new piece of content, it will feel jarring to your community—as if they sat down to watch *Law & Order* and ended up being shown *Brooklyn 99*. Even if they like cop shows, a thirty-minute comedy isn't remotely comparable to *Law & Order*.

Trust, shaken.

EXPECTATIONS ARE YOUR FRIENDS

One of the things that helped me gain my parents' trust as a kid was understanding their expectations so I could meet them consistently. They wanted me to clean my room? I did it—and I knew that meant folding my laundry and putting all my toys away. They wanted me to set the table? I knew that meant getting plates, silverware, and glasses for the family, so I made sure to ask everyone what they wanted to drink with dinner. I wasn't an overachiever by any stretch, but I knew what was expected and rose to the occasion.

You may have been taught to apply this same

principle in business management. When clear expectations are communicated, employees tend to perform better. They know what their roles are and how to fulfill them. They also know what happens if they don't. These types of guidelines are vital to long-term success.

The cool thing about applying the power of expectations to your Legendeered content is that you set the expectations as well as fulfill them. You get to decide what you will post, and when, and with what regularity. You get to decide how long your videos will be, and what they will be about. However, once you make those decisions, you have to be willing to stick with them.

Expectations and consistency go hand in hand. If you set no expectations for what you're creating, it will be hard to be consistent. If you're not consistent, your community will have no expectations—but they won't have any excitement or anticipation for what you're creating, either. If you only show up randomly, your brand will feel just like that: random.

One of the easiest and best places to set expectations is around the scheduled delivery of your content. You'll often see creators posting about their next scheduled content drop—"Visit our YouTube page every Tuesday for the latest episode!" This works because it creates consistency and anticipation by setting an expectation. Then, when the next episode inevitably drops on Tuesday, expectations are met, and trust is built.

I knew I was committing to a lot when I decided to do my daily Ironman training vlog (as I shared in Chapter Five). And, to be honest, there were days when I totally didn't feel like making a video—like the day of my accident. No one would have been mad at me for skipping a video day after breaking my collarbone in three places. But I had committed to a daily vlog, and I wanted to meet my audience's expectations. So, I showed up—sling, scraped face, and all. It wasn't perfect, but it was done. Expectations, exceeded.

There were a few other days when I couldn't post because I was at my parents' lake house in Canada with no internet access, but I still made the videos, and posted them (with a clarifying note) when I got back to civilization.

The thing most people don't realize about content creation is that, when you start sharing content regularly, you become like a friend to your community. And what are the most important things friends do for one another? Listen, and show up consistently.

Imagine that you and your friend agreed to meet every Friday at 5:00 p.m. for happy hour. What would your expectation be? Well, first, you'd expect that friend to show up every Friday at 5:00 p.m. If for some reason they were unable to make it one week, you would expect them to alert you beforehand. But, if that person started out strong and then stopped showing up around week five, without a word, then suddenly reappeared around week thirteen like nothing ever happened? You would rightly expect some kind of explanation. You wouldn't put up with a friend like that.

This comes back to "It's not about you. It's about them." Consistency and expectations demand that you show up for your community like you would for your friends. If you can't meet the expectations you set for yourself, communicate the changes needed and then be consistent to the change. Even big brands are made up of humans, and none of us will be perfect all the time—but the closer we can come to consistency, the more trust we will gain.

We'll talk more about the specifics of how and when to schedule your content in Part II, but for now, consider this question: what expectations can you set that will allow you to show up as consistently for your community as you would for your friends?

Consistency is a Long-Term Game

Before we wrap up this chapter and Part I of this book, I want to address the obvious and looming obstacle that so many people perceive when they begin Legendeering their content.

Legendeering feels like a lot of work—in part because of the philosophy, which is a departure from modern norms, and in part because creating long-form episodic video content does take time and effort. You may be wondering, "Will it really be worth it? Aren't there hacks and shortcuts out there that will get me the results in half the time?"

As I've said from the beginning, this is not a short-term strategy. It's not a sand dune; it's a mountain. Sand dunes are a short climb, and they feel tall in comparison to the surrounding landscape. But you can't build on sand. As quickly as you clamber up, you can slide back down again.

So many marketing strategies try to make sand dunes look preferable. "Reach this peak in one big step," they say. "It's easy if you follow my propri-etary formula!" Inevitably, those strategies shift and crumble because they're not built on sustainable principles.

On the other hand, you *can* build on mountains— and you can climb them, one step at a time, as long as you understand the path and don't expect to make the leap to the summit in a single bound. Mountains are a long-term game. But once you're at the top, you're there to stay. Sure, there might be a few storms, but with the right foundation and the right community, you'll weather them all.

Legendeering is a mountain, not a sand dune. It's a marathon, not a sprint. If you consistently deliver value to your community, you will create the founda-tion for a stable climb to the top. Just keep putting one foot in front of the other.

There is no such thing as an overnight success. There are no shortcuts in life or in business. Achievements take time—and using content to deliver consistent value to the community you seek to serve will also take time.

Don't panic, and don't push. Just be patient, trust the process, and move forward.

Shoot for the Stars

The reality of our modern culture is that most of us have multiple interactions with multiple businesses every single day. Mostly, those relationships are transactional: a given business has something we want or need, and, lacking a better alternative for acquiring it, we buy it from them.

However, the relationships we have with businesses that are not transactional—that feel human, caring, and personal—are the ones that actually make our lives better.

The ultimate goal of the Legendeering strategy isn't just to get your business visible (although it will do that), or to grow your community (although it will certainly do that). The end game is about changing the way we do business on a fundamental level, and to make the world of commerce—in which we all participate—a better place to be.

That's a big goal. Some would call it impossible. But I'd rather shoot for the stars and land on the moon by accident than never get off the ground.

So, as you move into the more technical chapters ahead, keep this larger vision in mind. By adapting your marketing to lead with value, always, and follow the five directives you've learned in Part I of this book, you are literally changing the way business is done, and how it serves. You are part of a global shift that will benefit everyone, everywhere.

I want to leave the world a better place than I found it. Legendeering is my contribution to that goal. Thanks for coming on this ride with me.

Now, let's go make some videos.

Video is by far the best tool
we have for building
authentic relationships
in the digital space.

Here's how to use it well.

PART II

LEGENDEER YOUR CONTENT

INTERMISSION

NOW THAT YOU understand the core values and directives behind the Legendeering strategy, it's time to put the philosophy to work in your business!

The Legendeering process unfolds in five phases.

- Phase 1: Development
- Phase 2: Preproduction
- Phase 3: Production
- Phase 4: Postproduction
- Phase 5: Delivery

Each of these phases covers a specific set of tasks that, when combined, can produce legend-making episodic video content quickly and consistently. When you follow this strategy, you will move away from the dreaded content scramble and into a smoother, easier flow where you always have a good idea what's coming next. (Remember, consistency is key!) More, you'll begin to serve your community in a new, value-focused way that will get them talking, create trust and authentic connections, and invite reciprocity at all levels.

I've structured this instructional portion of the book to be accessible to every business or content creator, regardless of budget, reach, or community size. If you're working with a whole video production team, what you'll learn in this section will help you communicate your goals clearly and keep things focused on leading with value, always. If your team consists of you, your iPhone, and your selfie stick, don't worry—I've got you covered, too. Even if you have zero experience with video production right now, you'll leave this book knowing how to craft compelling video content that creates massive value for your community.

CHAPTER SEVEN

DEVELOPMENT

Legendeering Phase 1

"THAT'S IT!" I yelled. "I've got it!"

Unfortunately, I wasn't alone on the trail. I probably looked like a crazy person.

Let me backtrack a bit. I had been tasked with creating a video for a nonprofit to help them with their fundraising efforts. The content was clear, but I just couldn't wrap my head around how to get it started. So, I did what I often do when my creativity needs a boost: I went for a bike ride on a local rail trail. Sometimes, we need a change of scenery to unlock our creative flow.

After my initial outburst, I thought about stopping to type my big idea into my phone. However, it was starting to get dark, and I didn't want to slow down. If I just repeated the script enough times, I reasoned, I would remember it, and I could keep riding.

I'm sure I looked (and sounded) like a complete lunatic, repeating the same lines aloud over and over as I plowed down the trail. When I finally got back to the trailhead, I stopped, pulled out my phone, and recited the whole two-minute script perfectly into my voice notes.

That video hit a nerve with the intended audience, and went on to raise tens of thousands of dollars for the nonprofit. I still share it as an example of powerful short-form content. And it never would have turned out so well if I hadn't been willing to look like a complete madman on the bike trail.

I guess what I'm trying to say is: developing your ideas requires a bit of courage.

In this chapter, we'll begin to develop the story ideas you've been playing with since Chapter Five, and narrow down a concept and format to get you started with your Legendeering video content.

Since reading Part I of this book, you've likely had a hundred (or more) ideas rolling around in your head around your own Legendeered content. In this chapter, we'll pin down the best of the bunch and help you map that one awesome concept to a repeatable, episodic format—starting with your overall concept.

Your concept is your starting point for the whole Legendeering process. It isn't one video, or one story; rather, it's an overarching "umbrella" idea that can be mapped to a clear framework (like the Four-Act Structure) and repeated over and over across multiple stories and topics. We also want whatever concept you choose to deliver clear value to your audience, resonate with you and your brand values, and be relentlessly authentic.

Ideally, you should be able to sum up your concept in a sentence or two. It should feel broad enough to be applied to multiple stories or iterations, but also narrow enough to clearly showcase your brand values and fill a value gap for your audience.

Landing on a concept is a bit like fishing. You need to cast your line a bunch of times, over and over, in many different directions—but when you land "the big one," you'll feel it immediately. There are more possibilities for Legendeer-able content than I could possibly iterate here—so the best way to coach you through this iterative process is through examples.

Let's start with *Law & Order*, the format of which we explored in Chapter Six. During the opening sequence of each episode, a narrator gives viewers a summation of the concept for the show. In the industry, they call this a "logline." For *Law & Order*, it begins like this: *"In the criminal justice system, the people are represented by two separate yet equally important groups ..."* This introduction is closely followed by the iconic *dun-dun* sound. Only after those two pieces appear does the episode begin.

That's the kind of concept summation we're looking for. It's clear and concise, but it sparks interest.

Here are some examples specific to Legendeering.

Remember Lyn, our Realtor from New York? Her concept could be summed up as, "An exploration of the history, significance, and benefits of green spaces in New York City with the people who preserve them."

Michael, the owner of an insurance agency, donates a significant portion of his profits to local charities. He defined his concept as, "Sharing how necessary spending—like on insurance policies—can create impact for local charities, and celebrating the good that our clients have already done through their contributions to those charities."

Finally, Alondra, a relationship coach, created a concept to "tell the stories of couples throughout the coaching process to show our community how to heal their relationships."

Your concept will be deceptively simple and also profound. You'll know when you've hooked it because it will feel right—you'll want to stand up and shout, "Oh, yeah! That's it!"

Find Examples and References

One helpful practice around idea development is to come up with a file of "References"—videos, images, and audio that reflect what you'd like to create. Basically, your References file is a digital vision board for what you'd ultimately like to create.

For example, if you love the simple intro for your favorite YouTube show, drop the link to that show in your References file with a note, "Love this intro." If you like the music in a particular clip, make note of the track name and the artist. If you come across a stock photo image that just screams "my video!" to you, grab it!

When you're ready to create your Legendeered content, this file will help you make key choices later in the process—particularly in preproduction and postproduction. If you're working with professionals, it will give them a much clearer picture of your style, likes, and dislikes.

Build the Structure

Once you've nailed down a concept, it's time to map it to a framework.

Most concepts will map beautifully to the Four-Act Structure. Of course, you'll want to tweak the details to fit your concept and objectives, but regardless of your topic, this is a great place to start.

Remember, at this point you're creating a repeatable structure under the umbrella of your concept, not plotting individual stories or topics.

Here's how our clients from the previous section mapped their concepts to the Four-Act Structure.

Our Realtor, Lyn:

- **Act I:** Introduce the green space and give location, context, and backstory.

- **Act II:** Introduce the key person or people working in and for that space and share some of the issues they are facing.

- **Act III:** Bring the issue/challenge to a head through the storytelling.

- **Act IV:** Show the person or people meeting the challenge and triumphing over the adversity in order to preserve the green spaces they are passionate about and how this serves the greater community.

Our insurance broker, Michael:

- **Act I:** Introduce the charity. Help viewers get to know who they are and the broad scope of their mission.

- **Act II:** Start unpacking what the charity does within their mission and why.

- **Act III:** Bring forward the greatest hurdles for the organization and get viewers invested in the mission.

- **Act IV:** Show the end results of the charity's work and the change they've made in the community with the support of funding through necessary purchases (like home and auto insurance).

Our relationship coach, Alondra:

- **Act I:** Introduce the couple and their goals.

- **Act II:** Learn what problem the couple is facing and why.

- **Act III:** Watch as the problem comes to a head and the couple is forced to make a choice or change something about their behavior (with coaching from Alondra).

- **Act IV:** Watch the couple resolve the tension and talk with them about what they learned.

Select Your Stories

The final piece in the development phase is to brainstorm all the stories that might fit into the concept and structure you've just established. If you've done a good job with your concept and framework, this should be quick, easy, and fun. Ideally, when you're done with your first round of story selection, you should have enough material for at least twelve episodes.

For Lyn, this would look like making a list of all the people she is connected to who play an important role in the preservation of parks in the neighborhoods served by her real estate brokerage. With a list of people and parks at hand, Lyn can then begin asking questions to focus in on the topics for each episode. In particular, what successes and challenges are these parks currently meeting? And what stories is Lyn passionate about telling within that scope?

For Michael, this would look like making a list of

the charities his brokerage currently supports and whom he'd like to speak with there. From there, it's easy to craft interviews that showcase the good works of each charity and clearly illustrate the positive impact these charities have on the communities or individuals that they serve.

For Alondra, this would look like selecting willing couples from her client list and building out a framework for coaching them as they play out their relationship drama on camera.

So, get out your pen and paper, or open a note on your smartphone, and start jotting down ideas! You'll be surprised how quickly they accumulate. Again, you'll want at least a dozen before you move on to the preproduction step in Chapter Eight.

Congratulations. You now have twelve (or more) clear episodes of compelling content to work with.

Development Do's and Don'ts

Do remember the value gap

Remember: It's not about you. It's about them. No matter how cool your idea is, if it's not filling a value gap for your audience, it won't be as effective at building (and retaining) your community.

A good way to frame this is to think of each episode as a gift. Not a huge, splashy, special-occasion gift, but rather a small but practical gift, like those we sometimes receive from those who know us best, for no reason other than "I saw this, and I thought of you." Each episode of your Legendeered content should leave your audience feeling like they have been the beneficiaries of your consideration, for no other reason than that you care about them.

Do follow your passions

Some of the coolest content comes from an unexpected combination of topics or stories. So once you've identified the value gap, marry it with what you're passionate about. What will emerge is a viewpoint and conversation that is unique to your brand.

It's easy to confuse information with passion. Often, the business owners I work with get hung up on the idea of choosing topics based on the things they have a lot of information about—but the things they are actually passionate about have nothing to do with these industry minutiae. Unless those kinds of details *really* light you up, my suggestion is to prioritize your joy over cementing your expertise. Passion is contagious, and we all love a good story, so focus on the things you care deeply about instead of things you know a lot about.

Do be willing to ideate ... a lot

The first thing we think of when it comes to any subject is something we've heard about or done before—which means it's usually generic, overused, and possibly boring. There's nothing wrong with this; it happens to us all. Our brains like easy answers, and dislike deep thinking. Creative thinking is hard work.

Because of the brain's predisposition to latch on to surface-level ideas on the first go-around, it's vital not to get attached to the first story, idea, or conversation that comes to mind when you sit down to design your content. Absolutely keep track of the ideas you like—but don't stop at the first good one! Be willing to continue the ideation process until you literally exhaust every single scrap of an idea within yourself, and then some. You'll be amazed at what can come through when you are willing to keep going.

A fun way to approach your concept and story topics is to brainstorm with a partner—particularly someone who knows your brand and value structure well. Just take turns blurting out ideas for ten to twenty minutes (or more). Don't censor yourself; the more bogus, the better! Creativity isn't a linear path, so wander freely until you hit on the gold.

Don't chase followers or views

What Nielsen ratings are to television, followers and views are to social media. The obsession with these numbers is a direct carry-over from the television industry and how networks use "viewer numbers" and Nielsen ratings to sell ad space. As we explored in Chapter Two, these are junk metrics.

Likes (or hearts, or claps) are somewhat better because they require action—but, in the end, they still don't measure the two factors that actually matter when it comes to marketing: impact and value.

Letting go of our attachment to audience size can feel challenging. We've been told over and over by savvy marketers that follower/subscriber numbers directly predict and influence our level of success. However, this is demonstrably untrue. It doesn't matter how many people see your stuff if they don't care about it (or you). Case in point: I've seen a bajillion ads for Budweiser in my lifetime. I love their Superbowl commercials with those lovable Clydesdales. I see multiple "impressions" of their products across multiple mediums every single day of my life. So what? I still don't drink their beer.

Big brands are figuring this out, which is why many of them are moving away from partnerships with celebrity-level influencers and toward micro-influencers—meaning, people with smaller but highly engaged communities. So, don't worry if your audience is tiny right now. Two thousand people who actually care about you and what you're doing will support you far more powerfully, and for longer, than a million people who don't give a crap.

Don't chase trends

In my Clubhouse room recently, a member of my community asked about using trending music in his video content.

"I started using that song that everyone's in love

with," he told me. "My views doubled overnight. But then, all of a sudden, my views were right back to where they were before. Was it an algorithm change? Is there any way to prevent that from happening?"

It could have been the algorithm, sure. However, the drop in views most likely occurred because all those viewers weren't coming for what *he* had created. They were coming for the trending song. And because they didn't come to see what he had created, as soon as that song stopped trending, the views stopped coming. They disappeared because trends change all the time, so once you start chasing trends to get views, you will have to continue chasing trends to continue getting views.

Other people's content can't build you an aligned community. And, let's face it, most trends are based on other people's content. So, unless your plan is to *keep* chasing trends and build a community around always being on top of the latest trends, I'd advise against ever getting on that hamster wheel.

Also, if you're following a trend, you're already behind the curve. By the time a content fad reaches the peak of its popularity, it's already on the way out.

Finally, remember the core principle of Legendeering: "Lead with value, *always*." Unless a trend offers real value to your community, it won't increase their trust in you or their desire to reciprocate.

In the end, the ones who benefit most from social media trends are the platforms they're created on—because platforms make money by keeping people glued to the platform (and selling ad slots based on user presence), not by providing quality content.

Above All, Remember the "Why"

The ultimate test of your concept and episode ideas is the "why" test.

A lot of times, my clients will hit on a story or concept that they love, but which doesn't make sense for their audience—and therefore doesn't belong in their Legendeering strategy. Instead of arguing my point, I ask a simple question.

- Me: "Why this?"
- Client: "Because it's awesome!"
- Me: "But why?"
- Client: "Because I get to go here/talk to this person/make this cool sequence ..."
- Me: "But *why*?"

After a few minutes of this, I watch their faces change. I see them deflate. It's *so* hard—but it has to be done. Otherwise, the content won't do its job.

In Legendeering, there is only one acceptable answer to the "why" test, and that is: "Because it does X, Y, and Z for my audience." If you can't clearly articulate that outcome, you haven't yet landed on the right concept, and you'll need to go back to the drawing board.

I'll say it again: It's not about you. It's about them.

Now, that doesn't mean it can't *also* be for you. My Ironman vlogs, which I told you about in Chapter Five, were absolutely helpful for me. I used them to create accountability for myself during my training and keep myself moving during the moments when I wanted to give up. But they were also for my community. In my first video, I explained that my aim was to inspire others to take on a new challenge. Throughout the arc of my training, I received message after message from people who had taken my message to heart and done something new in their own lives. When I administered the "why" test, I had a clear answer—and that answer wasn't "It will be cool to point a GoPro at myself every day for 153 days."

The "why" test ensures that, above all else, the content you develop is intentional and that it leads with value, always.

The W's of Development

A good way to keep yourself on target with all phases of the Legendeering process is to continually ask yourself questions using the Five Ws—Who, What, When, Where, Why—and to be brutally honest in your answers. Below are the five Ws of Development:

Who?

Who is your ideal audience and/or the constituent members of the community you serve?

What?

What is the value you are delivering to your audience through your concept? How about in each episode?

When?

In what order do the stories/topics you've ideated need to appear in your episodic content? Is there a story on your list that needs to be told first in order for the rest of your episodes to make sense?

Where?

Are the people and locations you'll need to execute on your concept reasonably accessible for you?

Why?

Why does this matter to your audience, and how will they benefit from your content?

If the concept, structure, and episodes you developed in this chapter hold up through this line of questioning, you are ready to move on to Chapter Eight and the next phase in the Legendeering process: preproduction.

PREPRODUCTION

Legendeering Phase 2

IN THE EARLY aughts, I was on the crew for a popular renovation show produced by the BBC. We were planning a shoot in Texas at the time, filming a classroom redo for a teacher at a public school.

"This is so cool," I thought. "It seems like something local politicians need to know about."

Well, two of those "local" politicians just so happened to be President George W. Bush and his wife, First Lady Laura Bush. So, twenty-something me decided it would be a good idea to pick up the phone and dial the White House.

"White House switchboard," came a tinny voice.

"Hi," I said, nervously. "This is Tom Langan calling from the BBC in New York. I'd like to speak to Mrs. Bush's press secretary."

I held my breath and waited for a response.

"Hold, please," said the switchboard operator.

And just like that, I found myself on the line with the First Lady's assistant press secretary. I filled her in on what we were doing at the school and asked if the First Lady might be interested in appearing in the episode, since she was a staunch supporter of education initiatives. She agreed to inquire.

The next day, my cell phone rang. It was Mrs. Bush's chief press secretary, with whom I ended up having several conversations about the show, our mission, and the logistics of getting the First Lady to Texas when her travel schedule was already packed. I got a little thrill every time I picked up my phone and heard, "White House switchboard for Mr. Langan."

Long story short, the First Lady was extremely interested in supporting our show and the teachers who were benefiting from our classroom renovations—but she couldn't make it to Texas during our shoot dates, as she was scheduled to be traveling with her husband, the President. Still, it was a pivotal moment in my career because it showed me that guts will get you everywhere.

The preproduction process is all about preparedness. In this chapter, we'll sit down with your concept and episode ideas and build out all the pieces you'll need to bring them to life in video form. You'll map out exactly what you're filming, how you intend to film it, what you need to accomplish that goal, and who you'll need to get on board (and when). While this may seem like an excessive amount of planning (particularly if you've never done video before), I promise that, if you do the exercises in this chapter, you will save hours and maybe even days in your actual video shoots—and saving time means saving money.

Before we begin, though, I want to remind you that there are no cookie-cutter solutions in Legendeering. We have our core principle—"Lead with value, always"—and our five directives to guide us, but when we get down to the nitty-gritty of preproduction, the answers will always be unique to what you are creating. What you'll find in this chapter isn't a batch of easy answers, but rather a series of guidelines to keep your creativity pointed in the right direction as you build out a detailed plan for filming your Legendeered content.

It's also worth noting again that these instructions are relevant whether you're working solo or hiring a production crew. If you're working alone, this chapter will make everything about filming and producing your content easier. If you're hiring professionals, what you'll learn here will help you understand what they're already doing and provide insights so that you can effectively manage their work and integrate it with your vision.

What Do You Need?

Now that you've got your concept plugged into a format and have selected your episode topics (Chapter Seven), you're ready to start assembling all the people, tools, and tech you'll need to execute on your ideas.

So, get out a notebook and pen, and answer the following Ws for each of your episodes:

- **Who will be on camera?** Will it be only you, will you be interviewing others, or are you working with a group? Who do you need to contact and schedule to complete your episodes?

- **What do you need?** Do you need any special equipment? More than one camera and microphone? Lighting, a studio backdrop, screen, or other props? Special clothing, accessories, or makeup?

- **When do you intend to film this?** What are the dates and times you've selected? How much time do you have to prepare?

- **Where will this be filmed?** Do you need to get permission to film at your chosen location, pay a fee, or book a specific time frame? Will you need to arrange travel for you or others?

- **Why have you made the above choices?** Are they the most clear and simple choices for your episodes?

Map out all of the above for each episode you've designed. Even if it feels rudimentary and obvious, put one foot in front of the other, and get it all down on paper.

As you do this, you may notice that you can streamline or simplify some or all of your concepts to reduce complicating factors. There's a reason we use the word "production" to talk about complicated things. There are a lot of moving parts—and the more complex your concepts, the bigger the "production" to create them properly. So, try not to let your content ideas balloon out of control. Big and flashy isn't always better. Make this easy on yourself!

Questions and Answers

Now that you know what you'll need for each of your episodes, it's time to move on to mapping your content, starting with one essential piece: what is the question you're answering in each episode?

That may seem like an odd thing to ask. But knowing your story and topic and knowing what question you're answering for the audience aren't always the same thing—and you need both in the forefront of your mind as you move through the rest of this phase.

There are two kinds of questions you can work with. One is an *implicit question*, which is asked and answered through the story, dialogue, or content. Here are some examples of implicit questions that you can answer for the reader in your content:

- **For story-based videos:** "Will the hero succeed?" "What happens next?" "Will she actually *do* that?"

- **For review or commentary videos:** "Is [product, service, idea] going to be good or bad?"

- **For how-to videos:** "What do I need to know to get [result]?"

On the other hand, *explicit questions* are asked aloud on camera and answered through dialogue and interviews. For example, the narrator (you or someone else) asks a question that's relevant to the audience, and the interviewee answers. Or the narrator asks a question at the start of the video that the rest of the content clearly answers.

For example, back when Gary Vee was making his wine review videos in his dad's store, he was answering a question: "Is this wine worth drinking?" By the end of each video, his audience had a clear answer that not only guided their purchasing choices but also increased their trust in him.

Fitness YouTuber Nick Bare creates a wide array of videos to help people increase their fitness. From the title, description, and the first sixty seconds of each video, you'll know exactly what questions will be answered if you keep watching—like, "What should I eat while training for a marathon?" or "What are the best leg exercises in the gym?" Clearly answering a question in each of his videos helps Nick attract like-minded people to his community, because the very questions they're typing into their search bars every day are the ones he's answering.

Social media experts get millions of likes simply by answering the question: "How do I post videos on YouTube?"

So, before we move on, take the time to get familiar with the questions being answered in your content—both implicit and explicit. If you are doing interviews—even if you plan to let them evolve organically—write down some key questions now.

Finally, if you're not sure what question your episodic content is answering for your audience, take the time now to figure this out. Regardless of how you do it, your audience's questions need to get answered in a clear way in each episode—because if they're not learning, growing, or benefiting in some way, why would they watch?

Intro and Outro

When you're creating episodic content, you will also want to consider what you want to use for an intro and outro, and how the approach you choose will support your content. This is a great place to revisit your References file. What kinds of intros do your favorite shows use, and what can you learn from them?

For example, if you're doing an interview-style show or a cooking show, a la Brian Rose's *London Real* or Yolanda Gampp's *How To Cake It*, you might create unique intros for each episode using a clip of the interview or baking sequence, possibly with music. Then, all you need is a short, thirty-second introduction or overview reel that can be replayed across every episode.

Or, you might consider the *Law & Order* approach, where every episode starts in exactly the same way, creating a recognizable "hook."

There are dozens of ways to create a great intro for your videos. Again, unless you have professional support, keep it as simple as you can. What matters most is that your intro captures the essence of your content so that people will keep watching, and creates the consistency, familiarity, and anticipation that keeps your community coming back for more.

Your Shot List

Now that you know what question each of your episodes will answer, it's time to capture all of the relevant pieces in a shot list.

A shot list is an industry term used to describe a list of every camera shot needed to capture a particular scene in a film or video. In essence, it's a fully developed plan for how you will capture all the component parts you will need to tell the story you want to tell. You'll want a separate shot list for each of your episodes.

While these can get super complex for longer-form content like television shows and movies, we'll start by simply laying out the basics.

On a blank sheet of paper, make two equal columns. Label the left-hand column "What's on Camera" and the right column "Dialogue." Then, proceed to map out all of the "shots" in your episode.

What's on Camera	Dialogue

For example, if you were interviewing an expert in a library, you'd want to know where the camera was pointing for that interview. Is it pointing at you, then switching to the expert, and then back to you when you ask a new question? Does the frame capture both of you at the same time? Will you be adding voiceover or narration to certain clips (and, therefore, you'll need to worry less about the sound and more about the image being captured)? If you're doing a scene that involves Zoom interviews, is your screen set to "gallery" to see all speakers, or to "speaker" to capture only the person who is talking?

If you're doing a how-to, should the camera be focused on your face the whole time, or will you need different shots like product close-ups, shots of you using the products or method in question, or shots of other people doing what you're suggesting? Will you need screenshots from your computer, or still captures of different key components of the process?

Again, we're not looking to overcomplicate things here—rather, our goal is to clarify and simplify so when you actually start filming you know exactly what needs to happen, what shots you need, and when everything needs to happen.

Here's an example of a shot list for a simple interview video using one camera:

What's on Camera	Dialogue
Close-up (CU) of John	John introduces himself as narrator/host
Betsy	John introduces Betsy as guest expert
Wide shot (WS) of John and Betsy	Conversation unfolds
CU of Betsy	Betsy answers key final interview question
CU of John	John wraps up interview
WS of John and Betsy	Both shake hands and wrap up conversation.

As you may have guessed, even this simple shot list will require someone to be working the camera—

to zoom in and out and refocus during key parts of the discussion. Alternately, it could be done without a camera person, either by using three cameras or smartphones on tripods—one to capture the wide shot of both parties, two more for close-ups—with all three rolling throughout the entire interview, or by using a single smartphone camera looking at a wide shot of John and Betsy the whole time, and then zooming in on the speaker digitally in postproduction.

The point isn't how complex or simple we can make your filming process. Rather, it's about knowing exactly what you need to do to get the end result you want. Without that basic shot list, John might not have guessed that he would want three smartphone cameras pointed at the interview set instead of just one—but now he'll go into his filming day with the appropriate equipment and support to execute on his vision.

Going into a video shoot without a shot list is a bit like playing darts blindfolded. Sure, you can improve with practice—but one little turnaround and you're aiming at your best friend's head instead of the dartboard. Not good.

Of course, you'll never be able to fully plan out a video shoot ahead of time. There are always variables you can't control. However, your shot list will give you a framework to underpin your process, and it will save you a ton of time, money, and headaches. Believe me, you don't want to be hunting down an extra camera, tripod, or GoPro on filming day!

PS: If you'll be shooting footage for your intro and/ or outro, don't forget to do a shot list for that, too!

Your Call Sheet

A call sheet is another industry standard that makes everything about filming a video easier. Basically, it's a list of the what, when, where, and who of your video shoot. If the shot list is the creative map for your episodes, the call sheet is the logistics.

Your call sheet should include the following:

- Shooting times and your filming schedule
- Shoot locations, including contact information, addresses, and start/stop times
- Names, phone numbers, emails, and roles of everyone contributing to the shoot
- Anticipated weather conditions
- Nearest hospital or emergency center with contact information
- Equipment being brought to the shoot and who owns it

I know it seems basic, but you'll be amazed how helpful (and timesaving) it can be to have all of this information in one place and accessible to everyone— particularly if there are multiple people participating in the shoot.

If you are filming multiple episodes across multiple

days, do a separate call sheet for each day, and make sure everyone has access.

You'll thank me later.

SCHEDULE, SCHEDULE, SCHEDULE

Before you go out and start filming, you'll want to know two things:

- Are you able to film everything you need to film in order to complete your episode (or the part of the episode you're focused on that day)?
- Are you completing the necessary filming in the most effective and efficient manner possible?

One of the things a good film schedule will do is allow you to be efficient with your time. For example, if you've done shot lists and call sheets for six episodes at once, you may see overlap in film locations across episodes. If Episodes 1 and 3 both include shots in your local butcher's shop, you can set up your schedule to film both scenes on the same day, therefore streamlining your time and effort (and the butcher's). You can also rearrange shooting schedules easily and quickly based on the weather, or if site availability changes.

Equipment and Tools

I've said from the outset that you can do this process with a full camera crew, or nothing but your smartphone—and I meant it. However, there are a few vital and inexpensive pieces of equipment that will seriously upgrade your video quality.

Unless you're truly working with a $10 budget, consider investing in the following. (Note: aside from the first, all suggestions are for specific situations.)

- **A shotgun mic**. For under $50, you can purchase a microphone that plugs into your smartphone. Studies have proven that audio quality is a better predictor of how long people will watch a video than visual quality (I know, it seems backwards), so getting good audio is imperative. Plus, if you're filming wide shots or interview settings, your smartphone's internal mic won't work properly, as it's designed to capture voices and sounds from less than a foot away.

- **A gimbal.** If you'll be shooting on the move, a good stabilizer—otherwise known as a gimbal—is a great idea to minimize camera "shake" while you're walking or running. You can acquire a decent one for under $150.

- **A good tripod.** Don't count on you (or your friends) being able to hold your camera steady for any length of time. For non-moving shots, any movement can ruin a scene. For less than $100 you can get a good, sturdy tripod capable of holding your phone or camera at multiple heights and angles.

- **A good podcast mic.** If you'll be filming interviews remotely, get yourself a good podcasting mic that plugs into your computer's USB port. You can expect to spend about $100 on this, but it will dramatically improve your audio quality. Bonus: you can also use it to capture clear voiceover narration in postproduction.

- **Lavalier mics.** If you're doing extensive interviews and your smartphone camera will be more than three to five feet from you and your subject, look into wireless lavalier (lapel) microphones. This will give you more flexibility with your camera setup while still ensuring that you get great audio.

What you don't need

- **A ring light.** Unless you're filming close-up product shots or makeup tutorials, a ring light isn't the right tool for the job. Instead, find locations inside or outside your house with good natural lighting, or look to buy large, inexpensive, soft-source lighting.

- **A fancy camera.** A professional digital cinema camera is a thing of beauty—and can cost as much as a new car. But unless you plan on becoming a cinematographer, you likely won't use it to its full potential. Put that money into other things—like securing the perfect location for your shoot, bringing in your "dream team" of experts, or hiring a professional film crew.

- **To figure everything out on your own.** If you have questions about things we haven't discussed here, remember that you have access to a modern Library of Alexandria via the internet. Do a quick search for whatever part of the process you're wondering about (using, if possible, the industry terms I've been sharing throughout), and I guarantee you'll find valuable information.

Why Preproduction Really Matters

Preproduction is about thinking everything through to the point that it's a no-brainer on shoot day. You won't have to think about what you're going to do, or with whom, or when, or where—you can just show up and follow the plan. This is a great way to increase your confidence if you're newer to being on camera.

The world is full of things we cannot control, and production is no exception. Just like in many other aspects of our lives, we do have control over the level of attention we put into a project that matters to us. The work of preproduction isn't glamorous or exciting, but it is the foundation upon which your content will stand or fall. So, do the work, and do it to the best of your ability. Your community will thank you.

Preproduction Do's and Don'ts

Do lean into the details

Your best bet when filming Legendeered content is to plan in excruciating detail. Make sure you know exactly what you need, and where, and when. You can always cut something out after it's been filmed, but you can't add it in after the fact. If you don't plan and you miss something important (particularly when other people or hard-to-access places are involved), it might simply be too late.

Do be flexible

Plan in excruciating detail—and then be prepared to throw it all out when things change. Detailed preparation doesn't mean you can't be flexible; in fact, you *must* be willing to adapt and change details, or one little setback could undermine all of your hard work.

It seems counterintuitive, I know. But consider this: you can't change the plan unless you have a plan to begin with—and the better the plan, the easier it is to adapt.

Do make sure you have the right equipment

Like I mentioned above, having some simple extras can make a huge difference in the quality of your video.

Don't sweat the small stuff

It is inevitable that things will change as your production moves forward—don't get mired down in details that don't affect the overall outcome of the shoot. Plan in detail but always think big picture.

Don't make assumptions

It's easy to assume that other people involved in your production will understand your vision or everything involved with the filming—but you know what they say about assumptions. Make sure you communicate clearly with everyone involved in the project—from your interviewees and film crew (if you have them) to the friends who volunteer to help—and share your call sheets well in advance of the shoot day. You can ask everyone to acknowledge receipt of the call sheets to ensure everyone actually looks them over.

Don't be afraid to dream big

Even if you find yourself asking, "Who am I to ..." don't be afraid to shoot for the stars ... or the White House. Reach out to your dream interviewees. Talk to the coordinator at your dream location. Ask for the support you need—because if you don't ask, the answer is always no!

The W's of Preproduction

Who?

Who do you need to contact, interview, enroll, or hire to create each episode of your content?

What?

What equipment, permissions, and gear do you need to prepare for filming?

When?

When will each episode be filmed? What other deadlines need to be met?

Where?

Where will you be filming, and what actions do you need to take to ensure that things will go smoothly at these sites?

Why?

Why should your community watch the episodes you're planning? What questions are you answering?

CHAPTER NINE
PRODUCTION
Legendeering Phase 3

I'LL NEVER FORGET the day we got "invited" to a mobster's house for lunch.

We were in Vietnam, filming episodes of an international real estate show. That day involved a tour of a vacant house with the real estate agent, the featured couple, and our small crew of five—meaning, me, a "fixer," the camera operator, our sound person, and a production assistant.

A "fixer" is a cultural liaison who supports the film crew when they're operating in a foreign country. They help you navigate, act as a translator, and generally smooth over any cultural *faux pas* the film crew might make. Our fixer on this trip, Dai, was a friendly young man who was an absolute fountain of knowledge about the geography and history of the area.

Once we'd checked out that day's featured house and made sure everything was in order, we started filming. Then, unexpectedly, the house's owner showed up. Usually we discourage this, as owners tend to get in the way of the film crew and sometimes try to muscle in on key shots. Since none of us spoke Vietnamese, it was up to our fixer to communicate to the owner that, if he wanted to be present, he needed to stay out of the way.

Immediately, I noticed something was up. Dai, who was normally outgoing and confident, seemed overly deferential and uncertain in his conversation with the property owner. However, whatever he said must have worked because the owner stayed politely on the sidelines and quietly observd while we worked through our morning shot list.

Then, Dai approached me. "The owner would like us to come to his home for lunch," he said.

"Oh, that's kind, but we have a tight schedule today and I don't want to make the crew stay late, so please give him our regrets and let him know we'll be finishing up shortly."

There was no mistaking the fear that came into Dai's eyes.

"What's wrong?" I asked. "Is that a problem?"

"Sort of. He's not a person you want to say no to."

Dai explained that the property owner, who I'll call

Mr. X, also happened to be the leader of a local crime syndicate—the Vietnamese equivalent of a Mafioso—and that we *really* didn't want to offend him.

Needless to say, I changed my mind and agreed that lunch sounded great.

When we arrived at the owner's residence, we were escorted into a beautiful courtyard garden by quiet servants. A table was set up, and the staff immediately began bringing out dishes of steaming food.

Mr. X was somewhat of a film buff, and very interested in production. Through Dai, he asked me a stream of questions about life in the television industry. I couldn't tell if he had a hankering for fame or if there was an artist under that somewhat scary exterior.

At one point during the lunch, Dai asked me, somewhat nervously, to please remember to look at our host when speaking with him. I'd been watching Dai throughout the conversation because he was the one saying words I recognized. However, that was perceived as disrespectful. I kept my eyes firmly locked on the property owner for the rest of our conversation.

Our allotted lunch hour came and went, and the food was still arriving. Another hour ticked by as I kept up our stilted conversation. I got the sense that we were going to be there as long as the property owner decided we should be.

Finally, I worked up the nerve to say, through Dai, "We are very appreciative that you let us film at your property. However, we are still on a schedule, and as much as I'd love to spend the rest of the day speaking with you, we really have to continue with our work."

To my (and Dai's) vast relief, he waved a hand, Godfather style, and said, "I understand. Thank you for sharing this meal with me."

He asked if we could talk more about production; apparently, he still had questions. I gave him my card and promised him that, absolutely, I'd be happy to continue our conversation. Then, I got us out of there as fast as I could.

Thankfully, I was able to think up some ways to make up for the lost time, and we finished the day only half an hour behind schedule. Luckily, since we'd been so generously fed by Mr. X and his staff, we had some leftover cash in the budget for coffee and treats. For a film crew, a little caffeine goes a long way toward smoothing out bumps in the road.

Sometimes, during video production, you need to deal with a curveball. I certainly didn't wake up that morning in Vietnam expecting to dine with a mobster! However, our crew were able to flow with events as they happened because we had three things in place: a solid plan developed in preproduction, a willingness to roll with the punches, and a good sense of humor. Despite an absolutely unexpected plot twist, we were able to fall back on our plan, finish the shoot, and have a good laugh at the wiliness of fate.

When you finally get to production day, it's natural to be a little stressed. Twenty-plus years into my career, I still don't sleep well the night before a shoot.

You've spent a lot of time and energy preparing for this, and regardless of the scale of your production, there's a significant amount of time, money, and effort riding on the outcome.

Despite your careful preparation, something is *always* going to go off the rails. Just know that it's coming, and don't let it freak you out.

Well, now that's out of the way …

Preparing for the Big Day

By the time the day of your shoot arrives, you should have five key components in place:

- Your full concept
- Fully fleshed-out episodes
- Your shot list(s)
- Your call sheet(s)
- A working plan to get the most out of your time in front of the camera

When you come armed with those components, you have a plan. And when one or more of the many moving parts of your day needs to change—such as one of your interviewees is stuck in traffic, the park where you wanted to film is suddenly full of shouting bocce players, or the weather takes a nosedive—you can adjust the plan and salvage the day.

Remember, a plan can always change—but if there's no plan, you can't change it.

Here are a few more things to remember as you make the final preparations for your shoot:

- Pack everything you need at least one day ahead so you don't forget anything. This will also give you a chance to put hands on all of your equipment in advance to check for issues.

- Make sure all of your batteries are charged, and bring extras. Lots of them. (Alternatively, invest in a portable charging station.)

- If you haven't already sent them (hint: you should have), make sure everyone who's participating in the shoot has a copy of the shot lists, the call sheets, and any other relevant information. Don't forget to ask for replies acknowledging receipt of emailed docs.

- Go through your schedule and shot list to make sure everything is in place and ready to go for the shoot.

- Trust in the work you've put in. You have a plan in place, so now you just have to execute.

On Location

Woo-hoo! You're on location and ready to film. Whether it's just you, your buddy, and your trusty smartphone, or you have a full crew, there are some things you'll want to know before you get the camera rolling.

As with earlier chapters, this information is designed to be a crash course for beginners, and a refresher course for those with a bit more experience. If you're filming on your own, this information will help you get the best possible results using minimal equipment. If you're working with a professional crew, understanding these concepts will help you communicate your vision more clearly and understand the "why" behind what the crew is doing.

Let's begin with the most basic of skills: how to frame a shot.

HOW TO FRAME A SHOT

While short-form video—like TikToks, Instagram Reels, and Facebook Stories—often calls for a vertical (phone straight up and down, aka 9x16 aspect ratio) orientation, in general it's better to frame long-form content in the "landscape" (phone sideways, aka 16x9 aspect ratio) orientation. Think of all the episodic shows you watch regularly; whether on YouTube or your favorite streaming service, they are generally formatted to fit your TV's 16x9 aspect ratio.

This orientation may require some adjustment if you're filming with a smartphone, since the camera will no longer be in the center of the phone, but rather at one end. Do some test shots to be sure you (or the people you're filming) are looking at the camera lens and not at the center of the screen. Otherwise, it will look like you don't want to meet your audience's eyes.

Moving on ...

Other than the landscape orientation, the most elemental guide for creating images of any kind—whether video or still—is something called the Rule of Thirds.

Basically, the Rule of Thirds helps create visual balance within the frame. If you were to draw two equally-spaced vertical lines through the frame, and another two equally-spaced horizontal lines through those, you would get four "intersections" where lines cross. Following the Rule of Thirds, you should always place the subject of interest in your frame either on one of the four intersections or along one of the vertical or horizontal lines.

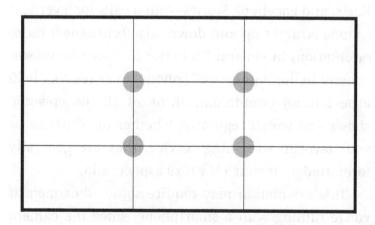

So, for example, if you're getting a wide shot of yourself talking to your viewers, you'll want to place yourself to one side of the screen along a vertical axis, and with your eyes or face along the top horizontal.

If you're doing an interview shot of two people seated in chairs, you'll want to place each of them along a vertical access with some space in between them (in the central column). A table or other dividing element in the center can provide good visual balance. Again, the top horizontal line should bisect their eyes or face.

If you're filming a shot of a bunch of people around a table, the tabletop should line up with the bottom horizontal line, while the top horizontal line should be at the average eye level.

Most well-composed video images use the Rule of Thirds as a guideline. It's not rocket science, but neither is it something you notice until you know to look for it. Now that you understand it, be prepared to cringe at the hundreds of posts in your social media feed that cut people off at the knees but leave eight feet of ceiling above them for no reason.

Most, if not all, smartphones and video cameras have a "grid" option that you can use to frame your shots. If you're filming on your own, use the timer to take some still images so you can test your positioning before you hit "record." These small adjustments can make all the difference in your finished product.

CLOSE-UP OR WIDE SHOT?

While making your shot lists, you may have noted places where you want the camera to zoom in for a close-up, and where you would prefer a "wide shot."

Now that you understand the Rule of Thirds, we can actually define what these terms mean so you know how to get the shots you envision.

In general, a "close-up" shot is where the subject fills the frame. If we're using the Rule of Thirds, this would put a person's eyes on the top horizontal axis, their mouth or chin on the lower, and their neck at the bottom of the screen. For a product or object, you would simply center the subject in the frame and/or focus on one key element or component.

A "medium" shot would be waist-up on a person— like what you generally see in a Zoom meeting.

A "wide shot" shows the full body, head to toe, with a bit of space above and below the subject. Alternatively, a wide shot might be a skyline, a natural landscape, or a full view of the object in question.

Obviously, the Rule of Thirds applies no matter what kind of shot you're setting up.

Generally speaking, you want to start any scene with a wide shot, because you'll want to establish geography for the viewer. For example, in an interview, you'll want them to understand that there are two (or more) people talking to one another in a specific setting. If you're filming in a natural setting, you'll want to show the full scope of the landscape. If you're filming a product or object, you'll want to show the whole thing before you zoom in on its component parts.

Once you have a wide shot, you can choose to stay there or go in for close-ups. In interviews, you'll often see a wide shot to show the speakers, then close-ups of the speakers during key parts of dialogue, then more wide shots to show the interactions between the speakers, then more close-ups. (As we discussed in Chapter Eight, there are many ways to accomplish this, including using digital zoom in postproduction.)

If you're showing your viewers around a park, you'll likely want to film the whole sequence in a wide shot, then go back for close-ups of key elements like statuary, benches, flowers, etc.

The shots you choose will reflect how you want your community to see the story you're sharing. There are too many possible sequences to talk through here, but here are two more ground rules to get you going:

- Film wide shots first, then go back for the close-ups.
- Never take the camera off the speaker. If you need additional shots of certain items or elements the speaker is pointing out, go back and film those after the fact.

WHAT ABOUT LIGHTING?

While you don't need to use studio-style lighting for your Legendeered content (unless you have the budget), lighting is important to make sure your content looks good. So, if possible, find a place with good natural light, and use it to your advantage, according to the guidelines below.

The biggest rule when it comes to lighting is that the subject should always be facing the main light source. That means, if there's a window in the room, you (or the person you're interviewing) should be turned toward it, rather than placing it behind you. If it's a sunny day, place the sun just slightly to one side of the camera, so you're not looking directly at it but it's still lighting your face. Partly cloudy days are great for filming because the clouds diffuse the sun's light and reduce harsh shadows—but too many clouds can make it difficult to see faces or details. If you're filming indoors, try to point the main light source at the subject—especially the faces of the people on film—and not directly over their heads.

A more robust setup would include what we call "three-point lighting." This means having three light sources—a key light, a fill light, and a backlight (aka a hair light). The key light is your main source of light—the brightest source that is doing the bulk of the work, which is lighting your subject. Fill light has lower intensity and is designed to "fill" the shadows created by the key light. The backlight is behind the subject, shining onto their shoulder, back, and side of their head; the idea is to put a little highlight on the subject to separate them from the background. It may take some practice to position everything correctly once you're on location, but the extra effort will be worth it.

Many websites sell simple three-point lighting kits. If you do choose to invest in lighting, buy the largest soft-source lights you can afford. The bigger the lights, the more adaptable and useful they will be across all of your filming scenarios.

There are so many variations when it comes to lighting techniques that it would be impossible to cover them here. However, if you understand the basics of three-point lighting, you will be able to position your subjects correctly and get the most professional-looking results from your footage. If you're doing your own filming and want to do a deeper dive into lighting, I've created a short list of helpful tutorials for you at www.legendeering.io/resources.

WHAT ABOUT AUDIO?

As I mentioned in Chapter Eight, audio quality is even more important than video quality. Here are a few tips to get the most out of your audio.

As we discussed in Chapter Eight, a shotgun mic is ideal when you're filming with a smartphone. You'll want to make sure that the mic is within two to three feet of you (or your subject). Since the lenses in most smartphones tend to have wide angles, this will usually mean a "medium" shot.

If you're doing a wide shot of an interview with two or more people, or if you're going to be walking more than four to five feet ahead of the person filming you, wireless lavalier mics are the way to go.

Regardless of your mic situation, you absolutely must do a sound check before you begin filming. Record a twenty to thirty second audio clip in the setting in which you intend to film. Then, listen to it back using headphones. If using earbuds, cup your hands over your ears to simulate earmuff headphones. If you hear any fizzing, clipping, echoes, or weird background noises, you'll need to adjust your setup. Be aware of your surroundings and listen for all the noises you normally tune out.

Early in my career, when filming inside a subject's house, the sound recordist stopped the interview because of an intermittent background noise. At first, we couldn't find the source of the noise, but after many starts and stops we finally figured out that it was coming from the refrigerator, which was plugged in on the other side of the living room wall. The sound guy marched into the kitchen and unplugged the fridge. Then, to my surprise, he opened the refrigerator door and tossed his car keys onto a shelf.

"That way I can't leave without plugging the fridge in again," he explained. I gathered, from our later conversation, that there had once been an incident involving the fully defrosted and terribly smelly contents of someone's freezer.

It's really worth some fuss to get your audio right. Faulty visuals can be corrected in postproduction with additional footage, still shots, or even lighting effects, but there's not much you can do to fix bad audio.

And, finally ...

HOW DO YOU KNOW WHEN YOU'VE GOTTEN A GOOD TAKE?

The best way to know when you're done filming is to consult your shot list. Did you get everything you had planned for (and then some)? Are you still missing something? Always fall back on your planning. It's a lot easier to archive extra footage than it is to go back and film another take because you missed some crucial element.

If you're not sure, watch the footage on your phone or camera. Do you like what you're seeing? Are you happy with what you've achieved? Don't fall into perfectionism, but do be discerning. Again, it's easier to do another take while you're already on site than to recreate it later because what you have doesn't work.

Above all, listen to your intuition. If your gut says, "Do it again," then do it again. If you feel like you've nailed it ... do it once more for good measure.

Production Do's and Don'ts

Do test everything

Your framing. Your audio. Your lighting. When in doubt, test—and then test again. Never make assumptions.

Do stick to the schedule

In the television industry, if you make people work beyond the agreed-upon lunch or dinner hour, you get billed extra—even on a non-union shoot. Even if your crew consists only of family and friends, it's still nice to run on time. After all, they're donating their time.

This isn't to say that you can't make adjustments. However, if you agreed to break for lunch at 12:00 p.m. and it's going to take you until 1:30 p.m. to finish your morning shot list, get everyone together to make a decision about whether to continue filming and eat late, or to pause and come back after your scheduled lunch. Making people a part of your decision-making can go a long way toward generating goodwill.

Do back up your footage

If possible, back up your footage to the cloud as soon as you film it. Then, save it on a physical hard drive or in another non-cloud location when you get back to your office. Always back up your footage in at least two separate places, and three if you can. When you've invested so much time and effort to get these shots, it's better not to take chances!

Do fall back on your preproduction planning

You put in all that work for a reason. Have confidence in your vision. That said, if you have a great idea on filming day, do it in addition to what you had planned, not in place of it.

Do have fun and roll with the punches

Producing your Legendeered content is a fun, creative process. Is it work? Of course. Can it be stressful?

Absolutely. Will random mobsters infiltrate your shoot and invite you to lunch? Maybe. But in the end, you're making something that's going to bring value to other people's lives. Have fun doing it—and do your best to make sure everyone with you is having fun, too.

Don't be afraid to do multiple takes.

The more choices you have, the better. Period.

Don't underestimate the power of snacks and coffee

I don't agree with Napoleon Bonaparte on much, but he was right about one thing: a film crew, like an army, marches on its stomach. People will go above and beyond for you if you feed them well—whether that looks like catered snacks and gourmet coffee on set, or pizza and a six-pack after the filming is done. If you take care of your team, they will take care of you—but nothing kills the mood faster than a "hangry" crew.

The W's of Production

Who?

Who are you filming with on camera, and who is the team helping you to bring your vision to life?

What?

What are the component parts you need to capture (on your shot list) to ensure you can create the Legendeered content you've planned?

When?

Are all the details, including days and times, laid out on your call sheet?

Where?

Are all of the locations clearly specified on your call sheet?

Why?

Keep your focus on the underlying reason for all of your Legendeered content: to deliver value to your community.

CHAPTER TEN

POSTPRODUCTION

Legendeering Phase 4

AS I SHARED in Chapter Three, my first job in television was as a production assistant. However, from the beginning, I was fascinated by the postproduction process. Not too long after I started with that production company, I was promoted to Postproduction Coordinator—meaning, I was an assistant to the supervisor. I would do whatever was needed to keep things running: scheduling, paperwork, coffee runs, and whatever else was called for.

During this time, I made it a point to try to hang out with the editors and assistant editors and learn more about the process of taking raw footage and turning it into a consumer-ready show. For a short time, after one of our assistant editors left, I took on an additional night shift loading video into the editing system a few nights a week. Even though this new responsibility had me working from 9:00 a.m. until midnight—plus a forty-five-minute commute on either end—I was glad to do it because I was learning so much. Editing is a skill set unto itself.

Later in my career, as a producer and director, I spent a lot of time in edit rooms working with the editing team to craft the final product. It was helpful to know how it all worked; since I could speak the language, I was able to communicate more clearly and get better results with the team.

However, I never actually edited any material that I considered my own until I began plotting my transition out of television. Once I started doing that, my whole perspective opened up.

What I've always known, but now fully appreciate, is that it doesn't matter how great your footage is. At the end of the day, if your editing sucks, the piece won't work.

I think about it like woodworking; more specifically, like building a piece of furniture. You've come up with a clear concept (development), planned and sketched how everything will fit together (preproduction), and then made the rough cuts for all the component pieces (production). But that still leaves you with an unfinished piece—and the finish you put on it will determine how people see it, how they use it, and how well it holds up over time. Postproduction is where you take the raw material you've gathered thus far and make something beautiful and useful out of it.

Rarely does anyone see or appreciate the care and attention that goes into finishing a piece of furniture. They don't see the time it took to fill the nail holes, sand all the rough edges, and buff in the stain. However, if you put two identical pieces of furniture next to one another, with one being finished and the other unfinished, which do you think will attract more attention? Which will be more appealing, and sell better? The finished piece, of course. Same goes for video.

Another way to think about it is to imagine a car with all the body panels and interior finish stripped off. Will it still work as a car? Sure. But would it look good? Would it be fun to drive? Probably not. No one wants to see all the mechanics unless they're actually a mechanic.

I'd love for you to think about editing in the same way you think about finishing furniture or putting body panels on a car. It's detailed work, and it's time-consuming—but in the end, you get to be in charge of what people see.

In this chapter, I'll provide a basic overview of the process of video editing. No one can learn how to be an editor from a chapter in a book; editing is a career, a craft, and requires thousands of hours of mastery. My aim is to teach you enough that you can fill in the nail holes, sand the rough edges, and give your content enough gloss so that your audience can engage with your work without being distracted by the splinters. You don't need to create a cinematic masterpiece to serve your audience, only give them content that speaks to them and is fun to watch.

As with every other phase in the Legendeering process, you can apply what you learn here to your own work or use it to better understand the workflow of the professionals you've hired. The more you know, the better you can communicate, and the better the finished product. If you already have some experience with video editing, revisiting the basics in this chapter might offer some value for you if you approach them with a "beginner's mind."

One more thing before we start. If you've never edited video footage before, or even if you have, please be fair to yourself in your comparisons. In other words, don't hold up your content against your favorite television or YouTube show, especially if this is your first round in the editor's chair. That's not fair to you. Embrace the fact that you are at the starting line, not crossing to the finish, and that you are creating something unique.

Comparison, more than anything else, is what stops people from getting started with video content. So, just don't do it. If you are truly inspired by another content creator and want your stuff to resemble theirs, go back to the very first videos they posted and, using what you've learned in this book, see if you can zero in on key elements of that production. Let go of any need to be "as good as" or "better than." Instead, be excited that the content that's been living in your head is about to come to life on your screen!

The How-To's of Video Editing

So, how do you get started when you've never edited a video in your life?

Here's a step-by-step process to help you navigate your first time in the editor's chair.

CHOOSE YOUR SOFTWARE

If you own an iPhone, you already have video editing software at your fingertips. Apple's iMovie is a great beginner's platform that's user-friendly and free. There are also numerous free editing apps for Android and Samsung that allow you to edit your videos right on your phone.

However, if you have a bit more bandwidth for learning, I'd suggest a desktop application. First, a bigger screen means you can pay more attention to detail. Second, desktop apps tend to be more robust.

Which application you choose will depend on how big of a learning curve you can handle. Vimeo and YouTube both have built-in editing software that serves just fine for basic touch-ups; if you use either as a hosting platform, this will allow you to keep all of your work in one place. More powerful but still newbie-friendly software like DaVinci Resolve and Descript (which also creates handy video transcripts) can be accessed in both free and paid versions. And then, of course, there's Adobe Premier Pro, which can be accessed as part of their Creative Suite: this is a common choice for professional editors but can be very difficult and extremely daunting for beginners to navigate, so unless you have prior experience with other Adobe programs like Photoshop or Illustrator, and don't mind spending several hours or days learning the ropes, I don't recommend it as a starting point.

I never recommend one software program as a starting point for everyone, because everyone works and learns differently. My suggestion, therefore, is to do some research on your own, test a few different apps using their free trial period, and commit to the one that feels the most user-friendly to you.

I have a list of software applications that have been useful to me, my friends, and my clients at www.legendeering.io/resources.

OPEN YOUR FILES

Once you've decided which software you're going to stick with, choose the episode you'd like to work on first. (I'd suggest the one that you believe requires the least work.) Import your files into your editing software so you can easily see and access each.

Don't worry yet about your intro or outro sections. You'll create and/or drop those in later.

DO A RADIO EDIT

A "radio edit" is a first-pass edit where you remove everything you absolutely don't need—like long pauses, setup tests, bloopers, do-overs, errors, and unnecessary or tangential dialogue.

To begin, take all of the dialogue pieces that you filmed for your episode and lay them out on your timeline. This might be several pieces or one long one. (If you have close-ups or other shots to supplement your main video, leave those for later.) What we're looking for here is a start-to-finish version of the audio for your piece—hence the term, "radio edit."

When you're done, you should have a pretty close approximation of what the audio for the piece will sound like. Now, we can build the visuals on top!

CREATE YOUR COVERAGE PIECES

Once your radio edit is done, you may notice that there are "jumpy" bits in your video—meaning, points where the visuals don't match up because you've cut out parts of the dialogue.

For example, if you were getting passionate about something and talking with your hands in one section, and you cut out a tangent in that segment, you may notice that when the next frame begins, your hands are suddenly by your side. It will be clear to the viewer that you jumped forward in time. Same goes for cuts where you're standing up and then sitting down, or when the background changes. In order to keep this from feeling jarring, you'll need to create "coverage" for those transitions—aka, overlays of additional video or images that bring the two disjointed pieces together. After all, you want your audience paying attention to the dialogue and message, not the disconnects in visual flow.

Some simple ways to achieve coverage are:

- Cut to a close-up of the speaker from a different angle.

- Insert footage of the subject being discussed (so you no longer see the speaker).

- In interviews, cut to a "listening" shot, where you show the interviewer listening to the speaker and perhaps nodding in agreement.

For example, if the speaker is talking about how shiny their widgets are, you could create coverage by cutting to a close-up of the shiny widgets. Or, if a speaker is sharing their parent's legacy, you could cut to an old photo of the parent that matches the time period being discussed. Just make sure that whatever you choose serves to further the story, rather than distract from it.

Once you've chosen your coverage pieces, lay them on your timeline over the original radio edit. Think of this as filling nail holes in your piece. Most video editing software is non-linear, meaning you can

move pieces of media around on your editing timeline at will. So, when you decide you need a coverage
piece, just drop that on the timeline in the appropriate place.

Once you have all of your coverage pieces in place,
you can then trim them to the appropriate length and
integrate them into the flow of the video. If you're
using still images for coverage, you'll want to add
some sort of effect to create movement, like a slow
zoom or pan. iMovie has the "Ken Burns effect" built
in; most software will have something similar.

Once you understand how coverage works, you'll
start to see it in every video you watch. Don't be afraid
to take ideas from content that excites you—but try
not to overcomplicate things for yourself.

WATCH IT AGAIN, AND AGAIN

Now that you've added all your coverage pieces, watch
your whole video several times to make sure the transitions are smooth and that it's all flowing the way you
want it to. Watch it until you know it by heart—and
then watch it some more. Once you're no longer distracted by the content itself, you'll start to see what's
really happening, and find ways to improve it.

Also, fresh eyes are important. Once you're ready,
show your work to a few trusted friends and family
members. Be open to their feedback, but ultimately,
trust your own vision. Only take advice that actually
elevates the end product.

CHOOSE YOUR MUSIC

Music in a long-form content piece is basically emotional support—meaning, it complements and enhances the mood of the piece. So, when you start looking for music, think about the emotional components and overall feeling and tone of it, not necessarily lyrics that match your video content. In fact, if you're putting music under dialogue, make sure you're using instrumentals where there are no lyrics at all.

You may or may not want music through your whole piece. If your piece has a lot of movement throughout, music as a constant backdrop can help anchor the message and create consistency. On the other hand, if you're doing an interview or how-to, you'll want music only in the intro, outro, and at key transition times, and if you do use it during conversation, adjust the level so it doesn't compete with the dialogue. (Note: some software programs have a built-in feature called "ducking" to automatically change music volume based on what's happening in the timeline.)

Licensing and Fair Use

When you're choosing music, you'll want to be sure it's legally available for you to use. Any music you use should be labeled as "royalty free for personal and commercial use." A lot of music—i.e., on streaming services—is considered free for personal use, but you need a license for commercial use (anything associated with your business, such as your Legendeered content). So, if you want to use your favorite pop song, you'll need to research how to license it and likely pay a substantial fee for use.

You can circumvent this by choosing music from royalty-free audio stock sites. There are dozens of good ones, and most will let you listen to audio clips without a subscription. Once you choose the piece(s) you want, you can subscribe to the site and download the audio files. I've compiled a list of popular royalty-free audio sites on the book resources page at www.legendeering. io/resources.

VOICEOVER AND OTHER AUDIO ELEMENTS

After you've added your main video content, your coverage, and your music, you may or may not want to do some voiceover work.

Voiceover is when you (or a narrator) is speaking over a portion of the video but the speaker isn't on camera. Think of the hosts of *The Great British Baking Show* talking you through the sections of the challenge while you're watching the contestants prepare. Or the narrator from your favorite movie trailer saying, "A long time ago ..."

You might use voiceover if:

- You're creating an intro that includes some description of the series and what you're trying to accomplish. For example, "In each episode, we'll have conversations with [insert subjects] on [insert topics]."

- You want to introduce a guest over non-interview footage.

- You want to explain something about a tour or product that didn't get explained in the core footage.

- Your episode has multiple segments, and you want to bridge them with a narrative.

- You want to wrap up the episode cleanly and the same way every time. For example, you might say, "Until next time ..." or "Put that in your pipe and smoke it," and use that narration over a graphic outro or your credit reel.

If you decide to add some voiceover sections, you'll want to be sure they're recorded as cleanly as possible. If you're doing this yourself at home, my suggestion is to take your shotgun or podcast mic, go to the smallest room in your home, a closet counts as a room, close the door and put a big blanket over both your head and the mic. This dampens any echoes or distortions caused by the shape of the room. You can record right into your editing software (that's easiest as you can actually watch the video while you're speaking). Or you can use the Voice Notes app on your phone and transfer the recording into your video timeline later.

CREATE YOUR INTRO AND OUTRO

Now that you've had a bit of practice with editing content, it's time to make your intro and outro according to your vision from preproduction. Your intro should be anywhere from thirty to ninety seconds, while your outro could be as little as ten seconds.

We'll start with your intro.

Save your previous work (it's amazing how often we forget that) and open a new timeline in your video editing software. Just like with your previous content, drop your intro footage in, find where you need coverage and secondary footage, and choose your music. Record any voiceover elements that you need, and make the whole thing as appealing as you can. Run it by a few people to see if they can get the gist of your content from the intro alone, or if any adjustments are needed.

Your intro is one place where you'll want to rely on your Reference material. What kinds of intros do you like? What do your favorites have in common? What doesn't work for you? Give yourself time and space to try different approaches, and even start over if necessary. Since this will be at the front end of all of your episodic content, it's worth taking the extra time.

Some people choose to hire an editor or production team only for their intro, and then edit their main content on their own. If you have the freedom in your budget to do so, getting help with your intro can really uplevel the user experience. Again, your preproduction plan will be highly useful when engaging professionals and getting the exact look and feel you imagine.

The outro is generally less complex than the intro—but that doesn't mean you should skimp on it. After all, it's the last thing people see before they switch off the content. A good outro is the mirror to the intro in that it wraps up what the intro opened. It could be a recap of what happened, a summary of lessons learned, or directions for viewers to get more information. I don't encourage anyone to put their website link at the end of a video unless the person watching can actually click on it. Same goes for your phone number or street address. Instead, put your logo or business name in the video footage, and all the other information in the video description with the appropriate hyperlinks.

After the outro, you can include credits, music, and other elements to wrap up the video. If you worked with multiple people to make this episode happen, it's great to give them some love at the end of the video. Then, to create and reinforce consistency, add a graphic at the end of the video to let people know when they can expect new content—for example, "New episodes every Thursday on YouTube."

Once you're done editing your intro and outro, export the video files. Then, open your episode file and drop your intro and outro onto your timeline.

FINALIZE YOUR VIDEO

We'll get into the details of how to export your videos in Chapter Eleven, where we talk about distribution and deliverables—but I know you want to see your video in action, so let's get it finalized!

Before you wrap up your postproduction, here are some final things to check:

- Make sure you can hear and understand all dialogue, conversation, and narration. If you can't, you can adjust the levels in your editing software to compensate.

- Make sure there are no "black holes" where you forgot to cover a cut or blank space on the timeline.

- Show the final version to the people you trust to give feedback. Is there anything you missed or that doesn't make sense? Don't be surprised if they find a few things last minute—when you've watched something a zillion times, your brain will fill in gaps and you will no longer see mistakes.

Above all, make sure that you're happy with the final product. It doesn't have to be perfect, but make sure you're excited to be associated with what you've created. Ultimately, it's your brand being showcased.

Postproduction Do's and Don'ts

Do be patient

Do practice patience. It's going to take time for you to become comfortable with the process. The first video you edit will take you a long time—but you'll get faster, and it will get easier, I promise.

Do back up your files in more than one place

As I mentioned in the Production chapter, you *must* back up your footage in at least two places, with one being non-cloud-based. You don't want to spend six hours on edits and lose them because you got locked out of your cloud account or they didn't upload properly.

Do ask for feedback

Show your work to friends, family, and colleagues at various stages of the process, and get feedback from them. Ask targeted questions—like, "Did that transition work?" or "Did that voiceover give you more clarity"—rather than general yes/no questions like, "Did you like it?"

Try not to let challenging feedback bother you. If it's coming from someone who's genuinely trying to help, flag it for consideration. Remember: It's not about you. It's about them. Each stage of trial and error will only make you better!

Do practice nonattachment

Just like in development and preproduction, be willing to let go of parts of the video that aren't working, even if you spent a lot of time on them. In the end, if something doesn't work for your audience, it doesn't belong in your episode. That doesn't mean it was a terrible idea, only that it doesn't work in this context. If there's something you *really* love that needs to get cut, consider how you might create a new episode that can include it in a useful way.

Do dress it up

If you get to a point where you feel comfortable with your software and the basics I've described above, feel free to play with graphics, animations, effects, and other "glitter" that can take your video from good to great. You can either outsource those elements or create them yourself. With some experimentation, you'll create a unique "look" for your videos that viewers will recognize and resonate with.

Don't try to make it perfect

Take it from someone who's tried: you will never make it "perfect." So, spare yourself the agony. Instead, ask yourself, "Is this the best I can possibly make this at this point in time?" If the answer is yes, you're done editing. If the answer is no, go back to the drawing board.

Don't give up

Remember that you have time. You can learn. You can do this. And the more you come to this process with the determination to understand it, the more creative and expressive it will feel for you. Your community needs to hear from you, so don't stop before you get your content out there!

The W's of Postproduction

Who?

Am I editing all of my footage? Am I outsourcing the intro, outro and/or graphics?

What?

What is the goal of the finished piece? Am I delivering on that promise?

When?

What is my postproduction and delivery timeline— when do I want to be able to share these episodes with my community?

Where?

Where am I distributing this content? And are all of the edits and exports optimized for the distribution channels I'm using?

Why?

Is all of the content on message and consistently delivering value to my community?

CHAPTER ELEVEN

DISTRIBUTION

Legendeering Phase 5

NOW THAT YOU have planned, filmed, and edited your Legendeered content, it's time to share it with the world.

So, where is your content going to be seen?

In this chapter, I'll share some ideas for repurposing your videos across multiple mediums so you can get as many eyes as possible on your central, long-form Legendeered content—and, by extension, your brand.

The Distribution phase, like everything else we've done so far, will require a certain level of technical proficiency. This chapter is intended to help you understand the different pieces of supportive content you can use to get your work out there, not to teach you all of the skills necessary to produce them. So, even if you did all of your production and postproduction on your own, you may choose to hire someone to help with this step. For the right person with the right skills, this will be easy work, and therefore relatively inexpensive to outsource. If you're already working with a production company, provide them with the information in this chapter; they should be able to produce the relevant pieces for you, or provide you with what you need so someone else can produce them.

If you're doing this on your own, my best advice is to be patient. Don't be afraid to experiment. Try, and try again. With practice, you can absolutely learn everything in this chapter, and even improve on it. Give yourself the space you need, and let go of your expectations. Who knows—you might even have fun with this!

Hosting your content

I always recommend that people upload their full-length Legendeered content to two places: YouTube and their website.

YouTube

While many people treat YouTube the same way they treat social media, it's actually not a social platform.

Rather, it's the second-biggest search engine in the world (behind Google). More, it's integrated with Google, so when people search Google for subject matter, YouTube videos are among the first items to pop up. In fact, if you value SEO and want to increase your ranking on Google, YouTube content is one of the best ways to do that.

People go to YouTube to learn and to be entertained—or, hopefully, to do both at the same time. While on YouTube, they're highly likely to engage with long-form content (like your Legendeered videos), and to watch more than one episode of a channel that intrigues them.

There are plenty of tutorials on how to upload material on YouTube, so I won't go into that here. (In fact, since YouTube is constantly updating its interface, the process will probably have changed again by the time this is published.) Before you export your video from your editing software, be sure to check YouTube's latest guidelines for video size and format. You can find the latest links at www.legendeering.io/resources.

Once you have your video uploaded, be sure to turn on the "captions" feature. Then, once the captions have been auto-generated, review them to be sure they're accurate. (You can edit them in the YouTube Studio interface if they're not). Pay particular attention to names and places, as those are often misspelled or turned into other words by the software.

Your Website

When people search for you (or your services) and land on your site, it's because they want to know more about you. Your Legendeered content gives them something to engage with that isn't a sales pitch, delivers amazing value, builds trust, and is all about them. Also, the more people watch your videos on your site, the more site views you'll get, and the higher up in the search engine rankings you'll rise.

Your website hosting platform may or may not allow you to host videos directly on your pages. If you can't upload your content directly, you can embed it from YouTube. (Your site hosting platform will have unique instructions about how to do this.) This has the added advantage of increasing your number of views on YouTube, which in turn increases visibility in YouTube searches.

You can also upload your videos to another hosting platform like Vimeo and embed them into your personal site from there. I use Vimeo because of the tools they give me as a professional, but most of the videos I have on my account are private and visible only to me and my clients. Making videos public on a site like Vimeo isn't likely to get you the exposure to your audience that YouTube will, because it's not a search engine—but if you're looking for better video quality, need advanced branding tools, or want to tap into a different creative community, Vimeo might be a good addition to your hosting spread.

All of the platforms have similar functionality in terms of video quality and automatically generated captions, etc., so pick the platform that best suits your needs.

Making your Content Work for You

In general, I recommend producing at least five unique pieces of content from each one of your long-form videos. Those are:

- Two forty-five to ninety second videos for social media
- One meme or graphic
- One GIF
- One podcast episode

While this may seem like a lot, it's actually quite simple to produce these once you have your long-form Legendeered videos edited and ready to go. In this section, I'll explain what each of the above is, how it works, and how to produce it.

SOCIAL MEDIA

I want to preface this section with a reminder that I am not a social media marketing expert. I'm a content production expert. So, we won't be discussing things like algorithms, the merits of one social platform over another, when to post, or any other strategy stuff. If you want to learn more about social media marketing, there are thousands of hours of free content out there to help you up your savvy. (Or, better yet, you can hire an expert and learn from them.)

That said, there are a few things you should know about how to use video across social media:

- **Short form is best for social content.** Unlike YouTube, where people routinely go to consume longer-form content, social sites encourage scrolling. So, instead of uploading your full Legendeered video to each social platform, you'll want to create a couple of shorter videos to get people engaged. Then, you can ask them to click through to the full video on YouTube or your website. Think of your social media videos as "trailers." They'll show the highlights of the full video to generate interest and make people curious enough to click through and keep watching.

- **Different platforms need different videos.** Every platform has unique ways of engaging users—and things are always changing. Therefore, the key isn't to lean into any one strategy, but to research what's working on your chosen platforms now. Before you create your short-form videos, decide where they will go; my recommendation is that you choose one or two platforms to concentrate on at first, and then expand your reach later when you've started seeing results. Each platform has its own guidelines for optimal video dimensions, size, and resolution, which can be found easily through a Google search. Make sure that you upload videos that follow these guidelines and are of suitable lengths for the platform in question.

How to Create Your Short-Form Videos

The precise method for creating your short-form videos will depend on your editing software, but here is an overview to get you going.

First, duplicate the timeline of your video so you have a unique file to work with. (You don't want to lose your original work if something goes wrong!) Then, watch your video again, and take some notes about what forty-five to ninety second section (or combination of sections) can stand on its own. For example, you could use one really powerful segment of an interview, or a series of funny clips or bits of conversation that add up to a full picture of your content. Just be sure that what you end up with makes sense on its own as an independent piece. You don't want people to watch it and wonder, "What the heck was that all about?"

Once you've chosen the section or sections of your video that you'll be working with, delete everything else on your timeline, and edit just that piece. You may choose to add a brief intro and outro to bookend the piece—but likely not your full video intro, as we need to keep things concise. If you are posting content regularly, your outro is a great place to advertise that—for example, create a graphic that says, "New Episodes Every Thursday" and include the name of your YouTube channel.

Finally, create captions for your video. Since most people scroll through their social feeds with their volume turned off, it's important to be sure that your subject and content are clear. Most editing software will have an option for automatic captions. Turn those on and embed your captions into your video. Then, just as you did with your YouTube upload, review them to make sure they're accurate and that all names and places are spelled correctly.

Now you're ready to export your short video. Many editing programs have features built in that allow you to change the aspect ratio to create square or vertical videos from your original content—but again, be sure to get the specs for your specific social media platforms so you can adjust your settings accordingly.

Once your videos are ready to go, upload them to your chosen social platforms. Put the YouTube or website link to your full-length Legendeered video in either the post or comments (depending on the platform's current best practices), and let it fly!

MEMES

Memes and graphics are another great way to drive people to your Legendeered videos.

How you create your memes will depend on your content and your audience. If you're doing serious or educational content, you could make a meme out of a powerful or inspiring quote from that week's discussion. If your content is interview-based, you could create a graphic using the show title and the headshot of the person you're interviewing. If your content is comedic and entertaining, you could grab a still frame from your video and make a funny meme from it.

Whatever you choose, just make sure that it feels aligned with your brand and the community you're building. If you're not sure, do some research to see what people in your target demographic are responding to. Don't be afraid to experiment!

GIFS

Many video software programs give you the ability to create GIFs. If your editing software of choice doesn't, there are also numerous online platforms that you can use to create your GIFs.

As you probably know, GIFs are useful everywhere—from unique posts on social platforms, to comments on others' posts, to emails. You'll get the best results if you choose a clip from your episode that is funny, interesting, or compelling—like you and your interview guest laughing, an outtake where you tripped over a crack in the sidewalk, or something else. Add some text on the screen for context.

Like everything else in this chapter, this isn't

meant to be in-depth instruction, only a push in the right direction. If you want to learn more about the science of creating GIFs, there are many helpful tutorials out there. You can find a few on the book resources page at www.legendeering.io/resources.

PODCASTS

When you hear "podcast," chances are you think "complicated." But it doesn't have to be. In fact, your Legendeered episodes can probably be turned into podcast episodes quite easily, with only a few tweaks.

First, you'll want to create a short audio intro and outro by combining music and voiceover that will be used on all the episodes of the podcast. For the intro, think of something short, simple, and descriptive of the show. For the outro, thank your audience, remind them of where they can find the podcast, and let them know when to expect new episodes. Listen to your favorite podcasts for inspiration about how to do a great intro and outro.

Once you have an intro and outro, create an audio-only version of your episode, removing any long silences (aka "dead air"). Bracket the edited audio with your intro and outro.

If your content is based around a single person (you or someone else), or is a how-to or tour style, you'll want to do some voiceover work to fill in any gaps in the audio. For example, if you're showing the viewer a piece of art, you'll want to paint a picture with words to describe what the viewer is seeing. Think of how NPR field reports are formatted: we hear a bunch of background noise, and then the reporter describes the scene in detail so we can "see" it before the information is presented.

Once you've edited your podcast episode, export the audio files and upload them to the podcast hosting platform of your choice. There are many free and easy-to-use hosting platforms available, and new ones are always cropping up. Just make sure whichever one you choose enables you to embed the episodes in your website, and that it reaches Apple, Spotify, and all of the other big podcast listening platforms.

Put It All Out There

Now that you have all of your various pieces of content ready to go, you'll need a plan to get them seen.

There are literally millions of ways to get eyes on your content, and the "best practices" for every platform are changing all the time. So, my advice is to come back to the core principle of Legendeering—Lead with Value, Always—and the five directives we learned in the first part of this book.

When you're putting content out there, consider the following frames based on our directives:

- *Give without expectation.* Share your work as a gift to your community. Don't put the pressure of expectation on your work, particularly expectations around sales. I guarantee that, with time, you will see the payoff—so be patient, and remember that this is about building trust. You're buying them dinner, and sooner or later, they'll return the favor.

- *Be relentlessly authentic.* As you share your content, be honest about what people can expect from it, and be true to yourself and your values in your messaging. Don't copy other people's hype messages in the hopes that they'll get you more views. Stay true to what you stand for—in your Legendeered content, and also in your social posts, podcast show notes, etc.

- *It's not about you. It's about them.* When you write social posts, share your memes and GIFs or write your podcast show notes to hype up your trailers, focus on what your community will receive from this offering. Why does it matter to *them*? How will spending fifteen to thirty minutes of their time watching your videos improve their lives? Once you know that, you've got the basis for all of your social media and email copy.

- *Start with story, follow up with facts.* Remember, it's the story that draws people in. Story gives them a reason to care about the facts. So even if your Legendeered content is super fact-heavy and intellectual, start by sharing the story of why it's compelling, not the nitty-gritty of what they'll learn.

- ***Consistency is key.*** This, more than anything else, is the core of a Legendeered content sharing strategy. Since you're creating episodic content, create a release schedule. My suggestion is to share one episode per week, and use all of the secondary content pieces we've created in this chapter to drive people toward that new episode. You can set up "new episode" reminders for people in your social feeds, as well as through email. If you are between episode series or don't have enough content to post every week, fill in with older episodes. It's much more important that you keep your promises to your audience than that you share new content every single week.

Distribution Do's and Don'ts

Do your research

You'll get much better results if you take the time to understand how people are using the social platforms you've chosen, and craft your assets accordingly.

Do back up your files in more than one place

I can't say this enough. You don't want a simple glitch

to cost you all of your hard work. Back up your stuff.

Do ask for feedback

Just as you did with your long-form content, ask people you trust for feedback on your short-form videos, memes, GIFs, and podcast episodes. How can you make them more exciting, appealing, and user-friendly? Again, don't let any criticisms get to you; you're on a learning curve, and there's always room to improve.

Don't assume all formats are the same

Not all distribution channels and social media sites will accept videos in the same formats, so make sure you're exporting your content in the right formats for the channels you've decided to use.

Don't play favorites

Just because you prefer one distribution channel or social site over another doesn't mean that's the best place to reach your community. Go where your community is, and deliver value to them where *they* are, not where you prefer to be.

Don't skimp on volume

Don't stop with one meme or one GIF per episode if you can easily create two or three. You can always use the additional content to fill in gaps between episodes, or to put a fresh face on "reruns" between content seasons or when you're taking a break from sharing new content.

The W's of Distribution

Who?

Am I handling the distribution, selecting channels, and posting all of my content, or am I outsourcing some or part of this workload?

What?

Am I using the right piece of content (trailer, GIF, meme, etc.) for the right distribution channel?

When?

Have I set a schedule for content distribution for my community?

Where?

What distribution channels do my community use the most, and am I using that info to guide my distribution strategy?

Why?

Am I accomplishing my goal of delivering value to the community I seek to serve and tying that value to my brand?

AFTERWORD

IN 1948, THE SUPREME COURT settled the case known as *United States v. Paramount Pictures* with an agreement known as the Paramount Consent Decrees, a historic piece of antitrust legislation aimed at the film industry.

You see, in the first few decades after motion pictures had been invented, film studios had made it a point to gobble up every company and niche in the industry—from writing and development to production, postproduction, distribution, and exhibition. This vertical integration meant that if you wanted to get your screenplay made into a movie, you needed to be "in" with the big studios. If you wanted to work as an actor, you needed to get a contract with one of the big studios. If you wanted to edit film, you needed to work for a big studio. And, as a member of the public, if you wanted to see a film, you needed to go to a theater—which, by 1948, were largely owned by, you guessed it, the big studios.

Essentially, the Big Five studios (Paramount, Metro Goldwyn-Mayer, Warner Bros., 20th Century Fox, and RKO Pictures) and the Little Three (Universal, Columbia Pictures, and United Artists) had unrestricted power over what stories got told, and by whom. Together, they controlled nearly 100 percent of the film media that was available to be consumed by the public. There was no indie film industry to speak of at the time, and the bigwigs were determined that there wouldn't be one. Some of the unethical and unlawful practices reviewed in the lawsuit included "block-booking," the practice of bundling multiple films into a single theater license to reduce theaters' ability to work with multiple studios, and overly broad geographic film "clearances" or licenses.

After nearly ten years of legal battles, the Paramount Consent Decrees were enacted as a settlement between the government and the various film studios to dismantle some of the vertical structures and protect fair trade in the industry. Although the studios of course retained a large share of the market (and the power), and the settlement stopped short of banning theater ownership outright, the defendants agreed to divest themselves of their theaters and stop block-booking and other practices that restricted fair trade. This opened the door for competition within the industry, and for actors, writers, and artists to work without being tied to a big studio.

So, why does all of this matter to you, and to your Legendeered content?

Because in 2022, as I was writing this book, the Paramount Consent Decrees were sunsetted.

You might be tempted to think, "No big deal. So what if Disney or Paramount buy up some movie theaters?" However, as someone who pays attention to the media space, I found this news to be concerning. With protections for independent filmmakers, content producers, and industry experts gone (unless new legislation is introduced), the big studios will go right back to annihilating the competition and edging out anyone who isn't already under their auspices.

In fact, it's already happening. As I'm writing this, Warner Bros. Discovery (the merged entity of Warner Bros. and The Discovery Channel) just killed a movie that had been written, shot, and edited, and was, by all accounts, ready for distribution. Why? Because they needed a tax break to help bolster their earnings report. They wiped out a *$90 million project* and hundreds of thousands of creative hours to protect their bottom line and make their shareholders happy. This type of decision-making—killing creative expression in the interest of serving the balance sheet—is just the beginning.

The more latitude big studios have to decide what media gets consumed, and by whom, the narrower the field of content, ideas, and expression will be available to the public. Less content will be produced overall. What *is* produced will be homogenized, because executives only like to spend money on a sure thing. Think superhero movies, crime dramas, and anything with The Rock. On the other hand, movies with cutting-edge or socially fringe themes, new directors, or unknown stars? Not going to happen.

If you look closely at the music and publishing spaces, you'll see the same dynamics at play. Labels only want artists who are *already* Beyoncé or Taylor Swift; they aren't taking chances on the people who *might*, with the right support, rise to that level. Publishing houses only want to work with authors who have already proven they can sell books; for nonfiction authors, the audience requirements can be outright ludicrous. In fact, this very dynamic was recently brought up in a new industry antitrust lawsuit, as Penguin Random House (itself the product of a recent merger) seeks to acquire Simon & Schuster.

Luckily, as individuals, we have many more ways of getting our content seen than media creators did in the 1940s. Between social media, a free internet, and the ability of anyone with a modicum of tech savvy and a few extra dollars to run Instagram ads, we are far better positioned to outlast the insanity that's going on in the big media companies right now.

And that's where Legendeering comes in.

You see, I think that the content creators of the future are not big media studios or starving indie artists, but businesses. We can fill the gap for our communities and provide massive value through entertainment and documentary programming. As networks and streaming services contract what they produce and showcase, businesses can step into the vital social role of sharing ideas that move people forward, create shared narratives, and, of course, lead with value. If you think about it, it's a tremendous market opportunity—if you're willing to go all in.

However, this new landscape will require more of us, as business owners, than has ever been asked of us before. It will require us to take risks and stand behind our values. It will require us to think differently about how we do business on both an individual and collective level, and how we create community around our businesses.

This—the diversification and personalization of content—is the larger purpose of Legendeering. It's time to put on our superhero capes and save free speech, freedom of the press, and freedom of expression. It's time to innovate, through the lens of service, what media and digital content look like. If we approach this from a self-serving place, the results could be disastrous. However, if we follow the directives of Legendeering, we can create real, positive change—while, at the same time, supporting our businesses, employees, and the whole economic landscape.

Innovation Is in Your Hands

While out on a run the other day, I listened to an interview with David Heath and Randy Goldberg, co-founders of Bombas, on the podcast *How I Built This* with Guy Raz. One of the topics was innovation and how it happens.

You see, innovation doesn't come from new ideas. It comes from the refinement and creative upleveling of old ideas. Nothing we know or use today was created out of thin air. Even groundbreaking inventions like the telephone and the computer were built using existing technologies in a novel way. The founders of Bombas didn't invent socks; they innovated a better way to make and sell socks in the current global market environment.

The same applies to Legendeering—and to you. As I've shared all along, content marketing as a strategy isn't new. Legendeering is innovative because of the principles behind it and how the whole model is put together, not because of any component part.

More importantly, Legendeering is adaptable. As you make and share your episodic video content, you'll begin to notice the nuances of your unique voice, style, and messaging. As I adapted the strategy of Legendeering out of nearly two decades in the television industry, so you will adapt your own strategy out of what you've learned in this book. You'll make Legendeering your own—and your audience will be served by that.

My sincere hope is that this book will serve as inspiration to drive you and your business forward into the future. Legendeering, from a visionary point of view, is about changing the way we communicate, and shifting the business/consumer relationship away from transactions and toward an exchange of value.

All of the most important relationships we have in our lives—with family, friends, mentors, and colleagues—are built on an exchange of value without strings attached. I believe that we can create those same kinds of relationships between our businesses and the communities we seek to serve. That is the ultimate goal of Legendeering: to transform the way we do business, improve the relationships between businesses and customers, and create a world where we work together to further shared values. *That* is the world I want to live, work, and do business in.

It might all sound a little "Kumbaya" from where you currently stand, and maybe it is. But the truth remains that, if we follow the core principle and five directives of Legendeering—if we lead with value, give without expectation, be relentlessly authentic, center our community in our communications, share our values through story, and above all, stay consistent—we *will* change the world for the better.

RESOURCES

To access any of the resouces mentioned in this
book, visit www.legendeering.io/resources

ACKNOWLEDGMENTS

WRITING A BOOK is a massive undertaking—always. No author reaches the finish line of holding a copy of their book in their hands without an immense amount of help from the people that surround them. These people, the ones who helped throughout this process, have my deepest gratitude for their unwavering support, their faith in me, and for helping make this book, this dream, come true. All of them, and now you, the readers of this book, have played a role in moving forward our shared vision to humanize the world of business.

I want to start by thanking my wife, Becky, who believes in me more than I deserve and whose honest guidance and feedback over the last few years has been invaluable. She makes me a better version of myself, whether it's by inspiring me to become an Ironman triathlete or by supporting my dreams no matter how unreasonable and outlandish they are. She is my favorite, and I am forever grateful that my demanding job led me to drink unreasonable amounts of coffee at Java Flats, where she was the manager and I was a regular.

My parents Tom and Christine Langan unwittingly played an integral role in this book. I was that annoying kid who always asked "why" to everything presented to me. In a pre-internet world, they often pointed me to the shelves where they kept a copy of the *Encyclopedia Britannica* to answer my incessant questioning, only to then be subjected to me sharing the things I'd learned. I was so obnoxiously inquisitive that I even disassembled the toys they gave me to understand how they worked. I know that my incessant curiosity was challenging, but my mom and dad always encouraged me to research and think critically, and they tirelessly fostered my desire to understand the world, and the people around me.

I am thankful for Bryna Haynes, my publisher who pulled this book out of me. Nearly two years ago, when Bryna and I first met, she told me that I had a book in me and that she wanted to be my publisher. If I'm being honest, I thought she was a little crazy, but sometimes it takes an outside perspective to be able to see the potential within and Bryna brought that exact and much needed perspective to this work.

John Parsley, my dear friend and an incredibly accomplished editor, who made time in his demanding schedule to read my manuscript and provide valuable insights.

Will Guidara, my high school classmate and friend who answered the call when I reached out for help despite years of silence between us. I am thankful for his generosity, and for contributing his keen insights to this book.

Geraldine Laybourne, whom I am privileged to call a friend, for her unwavering faith in this project and her staunch belief that the world needs this book.

Alok Appadurai for building the mastermind group that I joined which put Bryna Haynes and I in each other's orbit, and Hammad Abdullah for making sure that Bryna and I connected.

All of my colleagues from my time in television, and since, have shaped me, the Legendeering strategy and this book in more ways that I can count. I didn't plan any of this. Writing a book was never a life goal. Hell, I ended up working in TV by accident! But all of the experiences I have had over the course of my career, being on set, traveling the world and ultimately being trusted to lead teams of people to accomplish the impossible, have guided me to where I am today. I am forever grateful for those opportunities because they taught me so much, but most importantly, they taught me to believe in myself and my vision for a better world through better communication.

ABOUT THE AUTHOR

TOM LANGAN is a two-time Emmy Award nominated Director of Photography and Producer. With a career spanning over two decades, Tom has produced hundreds of hours of national and globally distributed programming for major broadcasters, including the BBC, NBC Universal and Discovery.

Tom has served as Showrunner and Series Producer on multiple complex and challenging projects, overseeing multi-million-dollar budgeted productions. He has staffed and led teams filming all over the world, in environments ranging from the Arctic Circle to sub-Saharan Africa, producing lifestyle, documentary, entertainment, and commercial content.

When Tom isn't working to Legendeer businesses, he pursues what might be described as an eclectic range of hobbies. In his free time, Tom is an Ironman triathlete, podcaster, volunteer firefighter, amateur chef and whiskey collector.

Tom and his wife, Becky, met on location filming with the United States Coast Guard in Alaska, and they live in New York's historic Hudson Valley. *Legendeering* is his first book.

Learn more about Tom at www.TalexMedia.com.

ABOUT THE PUBLISHER

FOUNDED IN 2021 by Bryna Haynes, WorldChangers Media is a boutique publishing company focused on "Ideas for Impact."

We know that great books can change lives, topple outdated paradigms, and build movements. Our commitment is to deliver superior-quality transformational nonfiction by, and for, the next generation of thought leaders, conscious entrepreneurs, creatives, healers, and industry disruptors.

Ready to write and publish your thought leadership book with us? Visit www.WorldChangers.Media to book your discovery call.

WORLDCHANGERS
M E D I A